CONTENTS

Preface

CONTENTS

BOROUGH BY PRESCRIPTION

A History of the Municipality of

TAMWORTH

BY

HENRY WOOD

Town Clerk, Tamworth

PUBLISHED BY TAMWORTH CORPORATION

1958

By the same author

TAMWORTH BOROUGH RECORDS

GUIDE TO TAMWORTH CASTLE

Printed in England by
Hudson & Son Ltd., Birmingham 3

LIST OF ILLUSTRATIONS

PREFACE

IN WRITING THIS BOOK, I have not attempted to give a general history of Tamworth. That has been done by Palmer in his *History of the Town and Castle of Tamworth*, written in 1845, and also by H. C. Mitchell in *Tamworth Tower and Town*, published in 1936. I have not had the time to supplement their histories. Since I wrote my book *Tamworth Borough Records* six years ago, I have often thought it desirable that a history of the municipal development of Tamworth should be made available to those interested in the growth of the town in which they live. I have therefore endeavoured to trace the progress of the Borough from Anglo-Saxon days, and to collect all the material from municipal and other sources covering every aspect of local government in the Borough which is worth recording; unfortunately, most of the records dealing with the period of about two hundred years from the middle of the fifteenth century have been lost or destroyed and this leaves a gap in the municipal history of the town.

The map now published is not related to any particular period; in preparing it an attempt has been made to give an idea of what the town may have looked like at varying times between the Norman Conquest and the sixteenth century.

I wish to acknowledge the encouragement and support given to me by the Tamworth Borough Council in the publication of *Tamworth Borough Records* and now this volume; also, I congratulate them in readily accepting my suggestion some years ago that the Court Leet Rolls should be translated, at least in summary form as the cost of full translation would be considerable. This task has been carried out by Miss M. K. Dale, of the Institute of Historical Research, and it is due to her excellent work that I am able to give publicity to the interesting contents of the rolls, without which the picture of municipal life in Tamworth would not be complete.

I also desire to thank Miss M. J. Bygott, the Borough Librarian, for the valuable assistance she has given to me, most willingly, in the compilation of this book.

H. WOOD.

Tamworth, 1958.

CHAPTER I

GENERAL HISTORY

TAMWORTH derives its name from its principal river, the Tame,
and the Anglo-Saxon word "worth," meaning a farm or
estate. Although the date of its origin is uncertain, it is known
that the town had become well established in Anglo-Saxon times.
There is no evidence, however, that it was in existence during the
Roman occupation of Britain, and it is unlikely that any will now
be found. Watling Street runs within a mile of the centre of the
town in its course from London to Chester, being midway at this
point between the Roman stations of Manduessedum (now known
as Mancetter near Atherstone), and Letocetum (now known as
the village of Wall). Tamworth, with its rivers, being in such
close proximity to this Roman road, may have then formed a
clearing in the vast Forest of Arden.

Shaw, in his *History and Antiquities of Staffordshire*, in referring
to ancient roads in the county, says "Wendley-way comes from the
west end of Tamworth church, runs on the west side of Drayton
Bassett park ; the other way it might have proceeded by Ashby
and Nottingham to Southwell." There is not much evidence in
existence to guide us as to the origin and purpose of this way. It
has been said that it was a saltway, known as the Upper Saltway,
connecting the Lincolnshire coast at Saltfleet with Salinae (Droit-
wich). Salt was a commodity much in use in former times for its
valuable properties in the preservation of meat and fish. Part of
this road would appear to be Salters Lane, which is referred to in
the Court Leet Rolls for 1294 as "Salterslone" and which ran
parallel with, and to the west of, Upper Gungate. When the London
and North-Western railway was constructed in 1847 it bisected this

1

lane, and the part to the south, slightly to the east of the present Cherry Street, was discontinued. It is not clear at what place this ancient road crossed the river. It may have been near Lady Bridge, for there was a ford at a point immediately to the east of the present bridge ; in fact, the old public way to the river still exists between the bridge and the car park at the entrance to the Castle Pleasure Grounds ; when the Borough Council enclosed the road and land belonging to the Castle Mill in 1909 they decided that such enclosure should be "exclusive of the ancient way to the river." On the other hand, the Rev. Henry Norris, in his handbook on Tamworth Castle, thought that the road probably crossed the river at the Broad Ford in Lichfield Road. Nor is it known whether Salters Lane was connected only to Aldergate ; if this is the Wendley-way referred to by Shaw as passing the west end of Tamworth church, it may have continued in a straight line to Church Street.

When the Anglo-Saxons invaded Britain, they penetrated the country by proceeding along the rivers, including the Trent, and in due course would arrive at its tributary, the Tame. If there were no Celtic settlement here at that time, it must be presumed that the invaders at last reached this locality and regarded it, with its confluence of the Tame and the Anker, as a suitable place in which to live. This presumption can be made in the belief that Tamworth must have come into being in early Anglo-Saxon days for Offa to make it his chief residence when he came to the throne of the Mercian kingdom in 757 ; it is most unlikely that he would have made this choice if the town had not already obtained a degree of importance.

The Anglo-Saxons created separate kingdoms, of which Mercia for a long time was the most important. It was formed in 585, the first king being Creoda. Its size varied at different times, owing to wars between the several kingdoms, and at one time it stretched from the Humber to the Thames.

Mercia grew in power. One of its great kings was Penda, who, like his people, was heathen. After his death in 655, the Mercians became converted to Christianity, and St. Chad, Bishop of York, created a See at Lichfield in 669.

In 757 a battle took place at Secundun, now called Seckington, a village four miles to the north of Tamworth, between the Mercians

2

and the West Saxons. The Mercians were defeated, and Ethelbald, who had been their king for nearly forty years, was slain by one of his own officers, Beornred, in a rebellion. The traitor was put to death by Offa, who then succeeded to the throne of his cousin and thus became the eleventh king of Mercia. His reign, also, lasted nearly forty years.

With the accession of Offa, Tamworth became a place of considerable importance. He came here in the early days of his reign, and built a palace which was described by Palgrave as "the admiration and wonder of the age." It is believed that this palace stood between the junction of Market Street and George Street, and the River Anker, probably near the present Market Street entrance to the Castle Grounds.

Offa, it is said, was a great friend of the church. He created an archbishopric at Lichfield as a rival to Canterbury and York, and he also founded the Abbey of St. Albans. It can well be assumed, therefore, that there was a church in Tamworth in his time, if not before, for he kept some of the Christian festivals, particularly Christmas and Easter, at Tamworth. From his palace here he issued many royal documents, including two dated 26th October, 781, which were witnessed by the Queen and four bishops, and it is reasonable to suppose, therefore, that the king and his religious visitors had observed the Christmas festival in a church in Tamworth.

Offa constructed a ditch to fortify the town. It was forty-five feet in width, with a raised bank and palisades. It is referred to in many old records and deeds as "the King's ditch." The Borough archives contain many leases of parts of the ditch as gardens in the sixteenth century ; traces of the ditch were discovered at the rear of Lady Bank in 1905 during building operations, and in Marmion Street in 1908 when sewers were being laid. Even as late as 1957 there was evidence of the ditch at the lower end of Marmion Street when excavations were being made near the Co-operative Society's dairy. In 1855 the Town Council resolved "that the King's ditch running on the north and east sides of the Hilly Field" (a field at the corner of Albert Road and Marmion Street) "and thence to Victoria Road be filled up." The ditch is also known locally as "Offa's Dyke," but this name should not be confused with that of the great dyke which Offa constructed on the Welsh border to protect

3

Mercia from invaders. The course of the ditch ran from the River Tame near Lady Bridge to the west of Lady Bank and Silver Street, to the east of Orchard Street, to the south of Hospital Street and Albert Road, along Marmion Street and part of Mill Lane, and thence to the River Anker across Bolebridge Street. The river formed the southern part of the fortifications. The part of the ditch which ran along what is now Orchard Street was called the Walfurlong, and a field adjoining was also known by that name.

Another feature of Offa's reign was the establishment of a mint, coins from which can be seen in the Castle Museum. It was Offa who first minted the penny, then a small silver coin.

Offa was a powerful monarch ; he gained the overlordship of the greater part of Britain by his conquests, and took to himself the title of "Rex Anglorum," king of the English. He entered into an alliance with the Emperor Charlemagne, with whom he considered himself to be equal. It is said that a plan by Charlemagne that his eldest son should marry a daughter of Offa came to nought because Offa insisted that as part of the arrangement his son should marry a daughter of Charlemagne.

Offa died in 796. It is believed that he died at Offley in Hertfordshire and that he was buried in the Benedictine Priory in Bedford, but that his tomb was swept away by the flooding of the Ouse. Offa's son Ecgfryth reigned only 141 days. After the death of Ecgfryth's successor, Coenwulf, in 819, the importance of Mercia declined. Coenwulf's son, Kenelm, who succeeded to the throne at seven years of age, was murdered at the instigation of his sister Kendrida, who hoped to seize the throne. The Mercians had a hunting palace on the Clent hills in Worcestershire, and from this the boy was lured to his death at a lonely spot in the forest.

Tamworth is again mentioned as a royal residence in several documents issued in the reigns of Coenwulf (796-819), Berhtwulf (838-852) and Burhred (852-874), the twentieth king of Mercia. Disaster came to Mercia during the latter's reign. The Danes invaded the country in 865, and in 874 advanced as far as Repton in Derbyshire, where they destroyed the tombs of the Mercian kings. Burhred fled to Rome. In 877 the Mercian kingdom came to an end, after an existence of nearly three hundred years, and became part of the Danelaw, the territory occupied by the Danes.

4

Tamworth suffered heavily in the invasion of 874, no doubt more than some other places as a penalty for the greatness it had acquired, being razed to the ground. Desolation must have ensued, for the town lay in ruins for nearly forty years, but there is no record of what happened to its people. Then came another notable chapter in the history of Tamworth. Soon after Mercia ceased to exist as an independent kingdom, King Alfred the Great bestowed the nominal government of it upon an Anglo-Saxon nobleman named Ethelred, who in 880 had married the king's eldest daughter, Ethelfleda. Ethelred became the Ealdorman of Mercia, an office created by Alfred to enable him to give more attention to his royal duties, the ealdormen acting as his deputies in the provinces. Upon the death of Ethelred in 912, King Edward the Elder, Alfred's son and successor, permitted his sister Ethelfleda to assume the government of Mercia.

With much justification, Tamworth proudly honours the name of Ethelfleda, known as the Lady of the Mercians, for it was she who, with boldness and courage, enabled the town to rise again from the destruction which had been caused by the Danes. Assisting her brother in his campaign against the invaders, she created defences commanding the Watling Street and chose Tamworth as a strategic point. She came with her army in 913, rebuilt the town and constructed the huge mound which remains to this day as her monument, and upon which the present Castle stands. The Anglo-Saxon Chronicle records that "Ethelfleda, the Lady of the Mercians, went with all the Mercians to Tamworth, and there built the burh early in the summer, and after this, before Lammas, the one at Stafford."

Ethelfleda erected a stockade upon the mound. This wooden fortress was the predecessor of the Norman Keep we see to-day. The principal access to the present Castle runs over a massive curtain wall ten feet thick, and is considered to be one of the finest examples of herring-bone masonry. Whether this wall was erected by Ethelfleda in whole or in part, or whether it was made by the Normans, is a matter which is still an argument for the experts.

The Anglo-Saxon castle probably stood near the existing upper lawns, Offa's magnificent palace no doubt having been destroyed by the Danes. The Lady of the Mercians, when she was not engaged with her brother, King Edward, in fighting the Danes, made it her principal residence, and here she died in 918, "twelve days before midsummer." She was buried by the side of her husband at Gloucester, in the church which is now the Cathedral. She left a daughter named Elfwynn, whom the people of Tamworth desired to be Ethelfleda's successor, but Edward the Elder, the uncle of Elfwynn, marching from Stamford to Tamworth, suppressed the attempt, took the girl into Wessex, sent her into a nunnery, and assumed dominion himself, at first with much opposition. It was not until a year or more later, after many struggles, that he was acclaimed as King by the Mercians at Tamworth. Elfwynn had resolved to marry a Danish prince, and her uncle feared that the carrying out of such an intention would result in his enemies obtaining power in the territory which had been taken from the Danes. Upon the death of Edward in 924, Athelstan his son, nephew of Ethelfleda, became king.

Athelstan has been described as the golden-haired boy who was looked upon with favour by his grandfather, King Alfred, who gave him a purple robe, a jewelled belt, and a sword in a golden sheath. The boy had been trained in the art of war and kingship by his aunt Ethelfleda, and must have spent some of his time at her castle at Tamworth, for he was only six or seven years old when she came here. Upon his accession he, like his predecessors, made Tamworth one of his royal residences. He desired to live in peace with the Danes, and entered into a treaty with Sihtric, king of the Danes of Northumbria. Athelstan gave his sister Editha in marriage to Sihtric, who consented, as part of the arrangement, to be baptised in the Christian faith. The betrothal took place at Tamworth, in the presence of King Athelstan, on 30th January, 925. Sihtric accepted baptism, but soon afterwards he left Editha and relapsed into idolatry. He died shortly afterwards. Editha spent the rest of her life in acts of charity and devotion. She was given by her brother, Athelstan, the castle of her aunt Ethelfleda, and founded a nunnery, becoming its first Abbess. Like her aunt, she ranks as a noble Anglo-Saxon lady, and her memory has been preserved as the patron saint of Tamworth Parish Church.

During the reign of Athelstan, who regulated the national coinage and ordered that regal money could be minted only in a town, the royal mint which existed at Tamworth was confirmed. After Athelstan's death in 939 Tamworth ceased to be a royal residence.

In 943 the Danes again invaded Mercia, led by Anlaf, a son of Sihtric by a former marriage. The Anglo-Saxon Chronicle records that "Anlaf stormed Tamworth and there was great slaughter on both sides but the Danes gained the victory and carried away much plunder." The town was destroyed for the second time, and lapsed into obscurity for over a century. There are no records to tell us how much the inhabitants suffered, or how long it took the town to rise again from its ashes.

Then came the Norman Conquest. William the Conqueror, claiming possession of all lands, granted some to his principal followers as his tenants-in-chief as a reward for their services to him but making the holders liable to render him service, and retained other lands for himself. Among these recipients was a baron hailing from Fontenay-le-Marmion in Normandy, a village lying between Caen and Falaise, where the Conqueror was born. He had performed the office of Champion to his king in his own country, and was the Royal Steward and Dispensator. His name was Robert de Marmion, and to him William gave the royal Anglo-Saxon castle of Tamworth and its lands (all of which were outside the Borough boundary), with other lands elsewhere including the Manor of Scrivelsby in Lincolnshire, requiring him to render service as his Royal Champion as in Normandy.

The Borough itself remained in the possession of the king. The burgesses paid to him a fee-farm rent of £5 per annum for the Staffordshire part of the town, and £4. 16s. 0d. for the Warwickshire part. It is not known when these payments began to be made to the Crown, but there is a record of payments being made in the reign of Henry II.

The payment of fee-farm rents by boroughs arose after the Conquest. Norman bailiffs appointed by the king were responsible for assessing and collecting the king's taxes. This system was regarded as a burden and an imposition by boroughs which had a certain amount of freedom in Anglo-Saxon times, and so the practice grew of paying a fixed annual sum by a town to the king in return for the restoration of its Anglo-Saxon privileges, such as the

7

retention of fines imposed by the court leet and freedom to elect its own bailiff or mayor. Even before the Conquest many boroughs, by paying a fixed sum to the king, had obtained market rights and control of trade. A township had its moot or town's meeting which, under a law of King Edgar, assembled three times a year. A patent roll dated 6th November, 1275, recites that the men of Tamworth in the time of former kings, by payment of a fee-farm rent, elected their own Bailiffs and were exempt from service at the mills of the manor of Tamworth.

In Anglo-Saxon days, there were three classes apart from the nobles or thanes—the freeman, or churl, who owned his small plot of land, the villein, who held his land for his lord, and the slave, who was a mere chattel. The freemen were grouped into tithings, each consisting of ten men. A number of tithings constituted "the hundred," which had its own court, presided over by the county sheriff, to try offences. The Warwickshire part of Tamworth was in the Hundred of Hemlingford, and the Staffordshire part came within the Hundred of Offlow. The tithing, led by an official called the headborough, was responsible for the behaviour of its members, and so acted as a surety or pledge to the king. The headborough had to produce offenders or, unless it could be proved that the tithing was innocent in the matter, the tithing would have to pay the fine.

This system of mutual responsibility was later called the frank-pledge. There were also merchant and craft guilds, membership of which was usually limited to one trade or calling. The borough or port reeve, the counterpart of the modern mayor, acted as the king's representative, as did the shire-reeve, or sheriff, in the shire. The laws of the frank-pledge were administered by the court leet, which also made local by-laws.

Tamworth had its weekly market, which is still held on Saturdays and is believed to have originated in Anglo-Saxon times. There is no doubt that it has always been held in the street which has for centuries been known as Market Street, although the boundaries of the actual market place may have varied slightly from time to time. In early days it must have been held on the site of the present Town Hall. There is a record of the market as long ago as 1204, when the Bailiffs of Tamworth (the Mayors) had to appear at the Staffordshire County Assizes because it was alleged that they had unjustly taken toll of the Knights of the County of Stafford for oxen and cattle, and the "men of Lichfield" also complained that tolls had been taken from them unjustly. Another record states that in 1392 the Earl of Warwick was commissioned "to take measures for quieting the detestable dissension and discord between the Bailiffs and Commonalty of the Town of Tamworth in the counties of Stafford and Warwick, whereof one moiety is held of us in burgage and the other moiety of the Earl of Pembroke, of the one part, and the commonalty of the Town of Walshale (Walsall) of the other, as to the exaction of toll and other profits of a Market held by the former on Saturday ; and to summon three men from each town to appear before the King and Council." The record shows that the market was held every Saturday. In 1541, Leland, the historian, whose visit to the town is referred to in the next chapter, noted that Tamworth had a celebrated market.

In the fourteenth century the Bailiffs and Capital Burgesses obtained several grants for specified periods giving them power to take customs of certain goods coming to the town for sale, in aid of paving the town.

It is believed that the division of the country into shires was in existence before the time of Alfred, but that he ordered a survey which accepted, and laid down in a more precise manner, the boundaries of the shires. Tamworth appears to have been situate in the two counties of Warwickshire and Staffordshire in those early times, and, in fact, remained so until 1st April, 1889, when the town was placed solely in Staffordshire. This is interesting, for throughout a thousand years the town was associated with both counties, and although the population factor determined its present location in 1889, nevertheless history proves that the association of the town with the County of Warwick was at least equal to that with the County of Stafford ; the castle itself was in Warwickshire, and the Warwickshire portion of the town had its own bailiff or mayor, and capital burgesses or councillors, until the time of Elizabeth I. The change in the county boundary is referred to later in this chapter.

In 1246 Henry III granted the Staffordshire portion of the town together with Wigginton to Henry de Hastings, a descendant of a family which came to England with the Conqueror. These manors were forfeited with all other possessions in 1266 by the next descendant, who sided with Simon de Montfort in the war of the Barons against the King, and on 28th September in that year they were granted by the King to Philip Marmion for life. This deed of grant is the earliest document in the archives of the Corporation. The manors were returned to the Hastings family by Edward I in 1279. One of the descendants was created Earl of Pembroke in 1339, hence the reference to this title in the dispute with Walsall previously mentioned. The Borough part of these Staffordshire manors returned into the possession of the Crown at a later date, and eventually to the burgesses by payment of a fee-farm rent.

The Warwickshire part, which, like the other, had remained in the immediate possession of the King from the Conquest, was granted by Henry III to Philip Marmion in 1266 in the deed of grant already mentioned, along with the Manors of Tamworth and Wigginton. Upon the death of Marmion in 1291 this portion returned to the Crown. It was granted to Baldwin Frevill in 1317, but not for long, for by Letters Patent of Edward II, dated at York, 27th May, 1319, the King gave this Warwickshire portion described as being "of the ancient desmesne of the Crown," to the burgesses, their heirs and successors, as they and their ancestors had held it, in consideration of the payment of a yearly fee-farm rent of £5. 16s. 0d., the former amount having been increased by £1. The original of this grant is not in existence, but the Borough possesses no less than four Letters Patent confirming it, these having been issued by Richard I in 1377, Henry IV in 1400, Henry V in 1414, and by Edward IV in 1467. The grant of 1319 confirms that the burgesses had held this part of the town previously, for it says : "To have and to hold to the same men and tenants their heirs and successors of us and our heirs for ever with all Liberties, Free Customs, Commodities, Profits and Easements and other things to the said moiety in any wise pertaining as they and their ancestors in times past have reasonably held the same moiety."

Before referring to the Borough charters, one or two incidents in the general history of the Borough should be mentioned.

The town received three visits from Norman and Plantagenet kings, who were entertained at the Castle. Henry I came in 1115 ;

Henry II, accompanied by Thomas à Becket, then Lord Chancellor and later Archbishop of Canterbury, in 1157 ; and Henry III in 1257. In an inquisition taken in 1330, in the time of Edward III, it was recorded that Richard de Wytakere and Ralph Basset of Drayton held of the king four houses in Tamworth by the service of finding coals and litter (the litter was used as the royal carpet) for the King's Chamber for one night whenever the king hunted at Hopwas and slept at the Castle of Tamworth. This service was attached to the Manor of Perrycroft. Perrycrofts, referred to in the Court Leet Rolls as "Piricroft," was the area lying to the east of Lower and Upper Gungate, consisting of crofts and gardens. Perrycrofts Lane ran from the end of Schoolmaster's Lane (Spinning School Lane) to the manor house north of Albert Road. The Manor was held by the lord of Tamworth Castle, but in the time of Henry II it was granted by Robert Marmion to William Fitz Ralph, and eventually it was held by Ralph Basset and Richard de Wytakere in moieties.

In 1345 the Church and a large part of the town were destroyed by fire, and it is recorded that the inhabitants petitioned for relief from their assessments to the king's taxes.

On the eve of the Battle of Bosworth in 1485, the Earl of Richmond's army encamped on the Staffordshire Moor, on the west side of the town, on its way from Lichfield. It is said that Richmond himself, being at the rear of his army, lost his way by turning into Coton Lane, eventually proceeding as far as Elford, where he stayed the night with his relatives the Stanleys, and that next morning he rejoined his troops, and caused an altar to be erected on the top of Tamworth Church to implore a blessing on his venture. In Shakespeare's *King Richard the Third*, Richmond tells his men that they are "Near to the town of Leicester, as we learn, From Tamworth hither is but one day's march," and Scene II of Act V takes place on "a plain near Tamworth." At that time the Staffordshire Moor would undoubtedly extend as far as the main highway connecting Lichfield to Tamworth, and so would be a convenient halting-place.

A reference should be made here to the two commons known as the Staffordshire and Warwickshire Moors, the former being just outside the old boundary of the borough on the west, and the other near to the old boundary on the east. Their origin is obscure, but

11

it is probable that they were in existence prior to the Norman Conquest. The Anglo-Saxons, in establishing their settlements, followed the methods to which they had been accustomed—a little community with its collective responsibility, the freeman or free-holder with his strip of arable land, and the common pasture, usually on the border of the village, where the animals were turned out to feed. When the manorial system was created after the Conquest, some commons were formed out of the manorial wastes.

When part of the Warwickshire Moor was used for the construction of the railway, it was stated that the common rights could be traced from at least 1309 ; it would seem, therefore, that the common is of very ancient origin, and this would undoubtedly apply in the case of the Staffordshire Moor also. In course of time, in a manner of which there is no record, the right of pasturage became attached to dwelling-houses, and thus we find today that the title-deeds of certain properties in the former Warwickshire part of the Borough (Bolebridge Street, etc.) still include rights of common on the War-wickshire Moor for pasturage, while certain properties in the old Staffordshire part (Church Street, Lichfield Street, etc.) enjoy similar rights in respect of the Staffordshire Moor. The boundaries of both commons have varied since those early days, owing to enclosures in the eighteenth century, and to exchanges of land due to the construction of the former London and North-Western Railway.

The Corporation became Lords of the Manor of Bolehall upon purchasing the Castle in 1897, Lord Townshend having acquired the manor in 1782. Warwickshire Moor would seem to be part of that manor, while the Staffordshire Moor is part of the Manor of Wig-ginton.

In 1584-5, the burgesses had to insist upon their rights in respect of the Warwickshire Moor. It is recorded in the Court of Ex-chequer : "John Tomyns and five others, inhabitants of the town of Tamworth, in behalf of all the inhabitants, being farmers and tenants of divers of her Majesty's messuages, lands, etc., showed to the Court that the Queen and her progenitors and the tenants and inhabitants there have from time immemorial used to have common of pasture for horses and kine belonging to the said messuages, lands, etc., in one waste or moor ground called Port Moor, other-

12

wise Warwickshire Moor, in Tamworth, viz., every burgage two kine
and a horse, and every cottage one cow and a horse, till of late Sir
Walter Aston, pretending to be lord and owner of the soil of the said
moor as part of his manor of Bolehall, has disturbed the said tenants
and fee-farmers to have common of pasture in the said ground.   An
Injunction was granted till the cause should be determined, but Sir
Walter failed to appear, and his tenants have brought 1,000 sheep
into the common, though they have never heretofore been kept there.
An Injunction is granted for the removal of the sheep.''   (1584.)
'' . . . It is decreed that all the inhabitants, tenants and farmers of
the Borough of Tamworth in the County of Warwick from whose
tenements the Queen receives any rent service or suit shall have and
enjoy common in the said Moor except for sheep, unless sheep have
been usually kept there.''   (1585.)

Another Lord of the Manor had to be opposed by the Corporation.   The Bailiffs and Commonalty claimed to be the Lords of the
Manor of the Staffordshire part of the Borough ;   William Comberford, who lived at the Moat House in Lichfield Street, and who was
Lord of the Manor of Wigginton, also claimed to be the Lord of
the Manor of Tamworth.   He demanded a right to proclaim the
fairs, and, to assert his rights, employed men to dig in the town.
This step prompted the Bailiffs to take action, and they sued him for
trespass.   They were successful in obtaining an injunction against
him on 21st May, 1599.

A ballad, published in at least the sixteenth century, and well
known at that time, tells of a meeting between Edward IV and a
tanner of Tamworth.   The tanner was returning on horseback
from Birmingham and was in the vicinity of Bassett's Pole when the
king, who had been hunting in the neighbourhood, asked him the
way to Drayton Bassett.   Edward IV is said to have actually hunted
there when Drayton was owned by the young Duke of Buckingham
(who was the king's ward).   The tanner took the king to be a high-
wayman, and declined an invitation to feast at Drayton.   The king,
seeking to play a joke, pretended that he was a poor courtier and
suggested that he should become an apprentice to the tanner, who
stated that he would be more likely to lose than to gain by his
service.   The king offered to exchange horses, but when the tanner
mounted the king's horse it bolted, and as a condition of the horses

being again exchanged the king demanded twenty pounds instead of the twenty groats which the tanner had charged the king. The tanner was unable to pay, whereupon the king summoned his retainers who had been in hiding, but he surprised the tanner by creating him an esquire instead of punishing him. Tanning was carried on in Tamworth in those days ; a yard off Bolebridge Street still bears the name of the "Tan Yard."

The plague was prevalent in Tamworth in 1626, as it had been in the previous century. The records of Warwick County Sessions for 1627 contain the following : "Whereas heretofore in the time of the great plague at the town of Tamworth in this county the Justices of Peace assembled at the then Assizes, upon petition of the inhabitants there and for preventing the further spread of that infection, did take order that the sum of £32 should be forthwith collected out of the whole county for relief of the poor and infected households there, the same to be paid by £8 weekly for one month and to be afterwards further continued as cause should require, and whereas upon notice given to this court at the Quarter Sessions following of the longer continuance of the said infection and the great increase of poor there by reason thereof it was ordered that a new collection should be made of £16 more towards the relief of the persons aforesaid to be weekly paid unto the officers there appointed for distribution thereof, forasmuch as this court is now informed that neither the said sum of £32 was fully paid in, but some remains still unpaid, and that the said £16 hath not been collected at all by reason of some miscarriage of the notice appointed to be given to the high constables of the said last order, by means whereof and for preventing further danger the persons trusted were compelled to disburse the same and are still unpaid thereof, it is now ordered that all the high constables of this county shall forthwith collect and gather within their several divisions their part of the said £16 according to usual rates in other taxations and thereof as also all of the arrearages of the said £32 make undelayed account and payment unto the Clerk of the Peace of this county that so the same may be paid to the persons that have disbursed the same whereof they are not to fail as they will answer their neglect therein at their uttermost peril."

Reference has already been made to royal visits, and, in another chapter, to the visit of Queen Victoria. The Queen also passed through Tamworth on 27th August, 1853, when she was on her way to Ireland, and the royal train stopped at Tamworth station, where her Majesty "partook of an elegant déjeuner provided by the Railway Company." The Queen was accompanied by the Prince Consort, the Prince of Wales and Prince Alfred. A resolution of the Town Council of 1853 reads : "That the Council attend at the Station in their robes to receive the Queen on 27th August on the occasion of her alighting at the railway station ; that the portraits of the Reverend John Rawlett and Thomas Guy, Esquire, with the town flags and any insignia of office belonging to the Council be placed at the disposal of the Railway Company for decorating the station ; the Council to proceed in procession preceded by the macebearer, the town banner and police officers."

The last royal visit was on 29th May, 1924, when King George VI (then Duke of York) unveiled the local war memorial at Tamworth Hospital.

Although boroughs exercised powers of self-government from early times by letters patent granted by the king, it was not until the fifteenth century that incorporation began to take place. In the reigns of Henry VIII, Mary and Elizabeth, the practice of applying for such charters increased. There is no record of the proceedings leading up to the granting of a charter of incorporation to Tamworth. Queen Elizabeth I granted a charter on 24th December, 1560, presumably upon the application of the burgesses. It recited that the town of Tamworth in the counties of Warwick and Stafford was an ancient market town and that the inhabitants, by the name of the Bailiffs and Commonalty, from time immemorial had held it of the Kings of England by the payment of a fee-farm rent of five pounds sixteen shillings a year and had enjoyed various rights, jurisdictions, franchises, liberties, immunities and acquittances as well by prescription as by several charters which had been burnt or destroyed. Tamworth is therefore regarded as a borough by prescription, "from a time whereof the memory of man runneth not to the contrary."

The charter constituted the town a free Borough corporate, under the government of two bailiffs and twenty-four capital burgesses "of the best and most honest inhabitants of the Borough."

The capital burgesses were appointed for life, with power to choose successors to fill vacancies caused by death, removal from office, or by dwelling out of the Borough for six months. The Bailiffs (the equivalent of Mayors) were to be elected by the capital burgesses on the first day of August, and were to serve for a year. Failure to serve in the office of bailiff rendered the person concerned liable to a penalty of twenty pounds.

The Bailiffs were appointed Justices of the Peace, and were given power to arrest, by themselves or by their officers, felons, robbers and malefactors found within the Borough, and to provide a jail. The appointment of two mace-bearers was authorised, each to carry a silver mace, for the purpose of making proclamations, arrests, etc. The charter also renewed the grant of a Market (which had been held since Anglo-Saxon times) every Saturday, and two annual Fairs on St. George's Day and St. Edward's Day, which had been granted by letters patent issued by Edward III in 1337.

Power was given to hold a Court of Pie Powder (the name given in ancient times to a court which met at very short notice, from day to day or hour to hour, to deal with offences arising in connection with markets and fairs because the merchants could not stay long), a Court Leet to review the frankpledges, make local byelaws and orders and hear prosecutions, and a Court of Record to deal with plaints of every description and to any amount.

Another charter giving further privileges and powers was granted by Queen Elizabeth on 10th October, 1588. This gave power to nominate a Recorder, and to elect a Town Clerk. It granted a third fair which became known as St. Editha's Fair or the Cherry Fair, held in July (now 26th July owing to the alteration of the calendar). It was ordered that inhabitants were not to be required to serve as jurors with "strangers" in matters occurring beyond the Borough, and that no "strangers" were to serve on juries, etc., within the Borough. It appointed the Bailiffs as "the Custodians and Governors of the Free Grammar School of Queen Elizabeth in Tamworth."

This charter appointed the Earl of Essex as High Steward of the Borough, no doubt because it was through his influence that it had been obtained. His mother, widow of the first Earl of Essex, had become the third wife of Robert Dudley, Earl of Leicester, who

16

Charter of Charles II, 1663

acquired the ancient home of the Basset family at Drayton, later to become the site of the mansion erected by the first Sir Robert Peel. The Earl of Leicester found it convenient that his wife should live at Drayton while he was obtaining favours at the Court of Queen Elizabeth, and the young Robert, the second Earl, often visited Drayton from his possession at Chartley. It appears that he took an interest in Tamworth, and his rapid progress at Court, where he appeared at the early age of 17, gave him influence ; he was only 21 when he secured the 1588 charter for the town.

A second charter of incorporation was granted by Charles II on 17th February, 1663. This merely renewed the powers and privileges granted in the two charters of Elizabeth I, but it is now called the principal or working charter, being the one under which the Corporation still derives such of its powers as are not included in the general municipal laws. The charter appointed James Compton, Earl of Northampton, as High Steward of the Borough.

Fifteen years later this charter had to be surrendered. Charles II had commenced a practice of issuing writs of quo-warranto against many of the municipal corporations, calling upon them to show by what authority they exercised their powers. The purpose was to bring them under the power of the Crown. Many towns voluntarily surrendered their charters to avoid legal proceedings, on the promise of new grants, for which, of course, fees had to be paid to provide more money for the king.

James II continued this practice with even greater vigour, and in the last year of his reign Tamworth received a writ of quo-warranto. The advice of the High Steward, Lord Weymouth, and the Recorder, Sir Andrew Hackett, was taken and the Bailiffs and Capital Burgesses decided to oppose the writ. A month later, however, "for divers weighty reasons it was advised with the consent of the Recorder to surrender the charter to his Majesty's pleasure." An instrument of surrender and appeal for a new grant was sealed and Mr. Bailiff Harding was given the task of delivering up the charter, the seal of which was taken off by the Crown Official upon surrender. The minute book records that on 1st August, 1688, this being the date for the annual election of the bailiffs, a new charter not having been received the retiring bailiffs were asked to continue in office but they refused, whereupon two other capital

17

burgesses were elected. A few days later Mr. Morgan Powell, the Town Clerk, "for the good of the Borough procured a new charter with the addition of two new fairs and divers other advantages whereby the government was by Mayor and twelve Aldermen." He himself was nominated as the first Mayor under the new charter, and took the oath on 10th August, 1688. It should be noted that the new charter designated the chief citizen as Mayor ; this was the only time for centuries, in fact until 1835, that the title of Mayor was used officially instead of Bailiff in Tamworth, although some other towns had the title in earlier charters of incorporation.

However, the days of James II as king were soon to end, and on 17th October, 1688, shortly before he was compelled to abdicate, he issued a proclamation, says the minute book, declaring that all charters whereupon judgment was not entered should be restored to the condition in which they were in 1679. The new charter was therefore short-lived ; the former charter was returned, and the two capital burgesses who had refused re-election as bailiffs a little more than two months earlier resumed office.

The constitution of the governing body of the town set out in the charter of Charles II, two Bailiffs and twenty-four Capital Burgesses, remained undisturbed until 1st January, 1836. Following the reconstitution of parliamentary constituencies as a result of the Reform Bill, there was agitation for the reform of the municipal boroughs. It was alleged that as most of the councils of the boroughs were self-elected (as was the case of Tamworth), many of them had abused their rights and had misappropriated corporate funds. A Royal Commission was therefore appointed to investigate all the municipal corporations in England and Wales.

The Commission eventually reported : "There prevails among the great majority of the incorporated towns a general and in our opinion a just, dissatisfaction with their municipal institutions ; a distrust of the self-elected municipal councils, whose powers are subject to no popular control, and whose acts and proceedings, being secret, are unchecked by the force of public opinion ; a distrust of the municipal magistracy ; a discontent under the burthens of local taxation, while revenues which ought to be applied to the public advantage are sometimes wastefully bestowed upon individuals, sometimes squandered for objects injurious to the character and morals of the people. The existing municipal corporations neither possess nor deserve the confidence or respect of his Majesty's subjects, and a thorough reform must be effected before they can become useful and efficient instruments of local government.''

Tamworth came out satisfactorily in the report which was issued in 1833 after the visit of the Commission to the town. The following extracts from the Commission's report are worth quoting :—

"There is every reason to believe that the Borough of Tamworth is a corporation by prescription. The town was the seat of several of the Saxon monarchs, and possessed many immunities and privileges at a very early period. Grants of tolls were made by different kings to the inhabitants under the title of bailiffs and commonalty. In the 16th century the town appears to have declined, and ceased to be considered a corporation. It was incorporated anew by Letters Patent of Queen Elizabeth, in the 3rd year of her reign, confirmed by subsequent Letters Patent of the 30th year of the same Queen.

"There are no Freemen of this Borough. Prior to the passing of the Reform Act the right of returning Members to Parliament for the borough was vested in the inhabitants paying scot and lot.

"The Magistrates are the two Bailiffs, the High Steward, the Recorder and the Town Clerk. A Court of Quarter Sessions is held in the Borough, but for civil purposes only. Authority is given by the charter to try for criminal offences ; the magistrates, however, do not avail themselves of this authority, but send prisoners to be tried at the Assizes and Sessions for the county.

"There is a Court of Record under the charter, in which suits of every description may be brought, and to any amount. This court has, however, fallen into complete desuetude, no suit having been commenced in it within the memory of man. The magistrates are constituted, by the charter, judges of the court.

"The cause to which the abandonment of the criminal jurisdiction of the court of Quarter Sessions, and the disuse of the Court of Record are ascribed, is the want of a sufficient gaol, and the wish to avoid the burden of erecting and maintaining such an establishment, which would be entailed on the borough in the event of the jurisdiction which has been thus relinquished, being exercised. In the opinion of the inhabitants, the additional expense would outweigh any advantages which might result from the holding of these courts within the Borough.

"The Police is sufficient. It consists of two constables and two headboroughs, appointed under the charter at the Court Leet, and of one special constable appointed by the magistrates according to an arrangement with the Vestry, and paid by the latter. There are like night patrol appointed and paid in the same manner.

"There is a gaol in the borough, but of a very inferior description. It is used only as a place of confinement prior to commitment ; prisoners committed for trial being always sent to the county gaol. It would be wholly unfit for the purpose of protracted imprisonment, and can hardly be said to be a fit place, even for the temporary confinement of persons detained, not for the purpose of punishment, but of safe custody alone. It is, in fact, a mere dungeon, being situated under the Town Hall. It consists of a single room with excavations in the wall, in which the prisoners sleep. There is no sufficient admission of light or air, nor any yard or place in which the prisoners may take exercise.

"The annual income of the corporation applicable to their general purposes may be stated at £147. 19s. 0d. The property from which this income is derived consists of (1) Four houses let at rents amounting in the whole to £91. This property has been possessed by the corporation from time immemorial. In what manner it was originally acquired is not now known. (2) A house let at £28, together with a pew in the church let therewith at £1. 1s. 0d. ; this house was purchased with money derived from the sale of another house. (3) Three pews in Tamworth Church, let at rents amounting in the whole to £6. 6s. 0d. (4) Various chief rents and ground rents, piccage, stallage, etc., or market money, amounting in the average to £10. These tolls were originally granted by King Edward II for the paving of the streets and repair of the bridges ; the grant was afterwards renewed from time to time for the same purpose, and finally confirmed by the charter of Queen Elizabeth. The corporation are liable to repair the bridge called Boll Bridge and part of the Lady Bridge, which liability doubtless arises from the grants just referred to. The income of the corporation is expended in the repair of the streets of the borough, in the repairs of the market hall, and of the bridges, and in the payment of the salaries of the serjeants at mace and town crier.'' (The appointments of the High Steward, the Town Clerk and the Chamberlains were honorary.) ''Taking one year with another, the whole income is absorbed by these expenses. The Chamberlains' accounts are inspected on the 1st August in every year. The income being small, the inspection of the accounts is in practice left to the bailiffs, but any members of the body might inspect them if they thought fit.''

The report then sums up the way in which municipal administration had been carried out :—

''From the description which has been given of the constitution of the borough, it is obvious that the governing body is wholly self-elected. It does not appear, however, that the power thus vested in the body has been in any respect abused. The vacancies which have occurred from time to time have been filled up from among the most respectable inhabitants, without reference to party or to political opinions. Neither does it appear that the corporation, either as regards the appointment of members of the body corporate, or the exercise of the elective franchise, have been subject to the operation of any undue local influence. It appears that the magisterial duties have been discharged with intelligence and integrity.

''The Corporation afforded every facility to this investigation. They gave notice to the inhabitants of the holding of the inquiry, but no complaints were preferred, or matter suggested for investigation. The absence of all complaint, together with the evidence laid before me, leads me to conclude, that the objects of municipal government have been satisfactorily attained in this borough ; that the governing body have been judiciously selected ; justice well administered, and the revenues carefully applied to public purposes.''

The result of the Commission's work was the passing of the Municipal Corporations Act, 1835. This enacted that in future all municipal councils must be elected by the burgesses, that accounts must be audited, and that all income of the corporation must be paid into a fund, to be called the Borough Fund, the surplus of which must be used for the benefit of the inhabitants and improvement of the borough.

Tamworth was one of the boroughs permitted to be continued by the Act of 1835, which fixed the constitution of the new governing body for the Borough at sixteen, consisting of a Mayor, four Aldermen and twelve Councillors.

The 1835 Act required such boroughs as desired to establish or continue a court of quarter sessions to submit petitions to His Majesty in Council. Tamworth did not submit a petition, so the Court ceased to exist.

The Borough was granted a Commission of the Peace in 1836. This was renewed in 1873, and again in 1877, but by reason of the operation of the Justices of the Peace Act, 1949, the Borough became merged in the commission for the county, the population being below the minimum then required to entitle it to a separate commission.

The Act of 1835 abolished the exclusive rights of trading where they had been in the hands of the freemen, trade guilds, etc., and abolished the right of admission as a freeman by gift or purchase. The benefits obtained by freemen had varied in different boroughs, some having rights of common pasture or profits from common lands, others having educational privileges or eligibility to benefits of charities. The Court Leet, which made the local byelaws and dealt with offenders, was composed of the freemen, who were required to swear their allegiance to the king. When the Act of 1835 abolished admission by gift or purchase, the freedom could then be claimed only by virtue of birth, servitude or marriage. As there were no freemen in Tamworth at that time, no persons could henceforth claim admission. In 1885 an Act was passed which permitted Boroughs to confer honorary freedom upon persons of distinction and persons rendering eminent services to a borough, but without any right to share in the benefit of hereditaments, common lands or public stock of the borough or of any charitable trust. Sixty-five years elapsed before the Borough of Tamworth took advantage of the powers thus given, for it was not until 8th January, 1951, that the first admission to honorary freedom was made. Upon that occasion Alderman Frederick George Allton was admitted in recognition of his services rendered to the Borough over a period of fifty years. A second admission to honorary freedom was made on 4th January, 1955, when the honour was conferred upon Alderman George Henry Jones, who, amongst other public work, had taken a prominent part in the introduction of electricity into the town, and in the development of the Castle Pleasure Grounds.

As mentioned earlier in this chapter, Tamworth, from the time counties were formed, was situate in two counties, Staffordshire and Warwickshire, until 1889. The county boundary ran along the Holloway, Silver Street, Church Street, Lower Gungate and Upper Gungate.

The Local Government Act, 1888, which created County Councils (prior to that year such administration as was controlled by the counties was carried out through the county justices) enacted that as from 1st April, 1889, any urban area which was situated in more than one county should be deemed to be within that county which contained the largest portion of the population according to the 1881 census, the purpose being to simplify county administration and to obviate the difficulties which would have arisen through two county councils administering services in one district. Tamworth was affected by this arrangement. The census of 1881 had recorded a population of 2,589 in the Staffordshire part of the Borough and 2,032 in the Warwickshire part. Therefore Tamworth automatically became wholly a Staffordshire borough for local government purposes as from 1st April, 1889. Except for the continuation of parliamentary boundaries for a time, the long association of the Borough with Warwickshire was ended.

For centuries, so far as is known, the boundaries of the Borough had remained unaltered. Until 1888, any extensions of local government areas could be made only by a special Act of Parliament; in 1835 a Municipal Corporation Boundaries Commission expressed the view that "some alteration should be made in the ancient boundary of the Borough, for the purpose of including within its limits portions of ground already built upon and which may fairly be called upon to contribute to a Borough rate," and they recommended a line as answering that purpose, which would have included part of the parish of Tamworth Castle, Kettlebrook, Bolehall and part of Glascote, but the Borough could not afford the expense of applying for an Act of Parliament for the purpose.

The Act of 1888 permitted local authorities to submit a memorial to the Local Government Board praying for an extension of boundaries, and gave the Board power to investigate any petition submitted and to make a Provisional Order, subject to approval by Parliament, embodying its recommendations. The Tamworth Town Council submitted a memorial to the Board in 1889 applying for an extension of boundaries so as to include therein all the townships within the Parish of Tamworth : Amington and Stonidelph, Bolehall and Glascote, Tamworth Castle, Wilnecote, Wigginton, Fazeley and Syerscote.

The Borough boundary at that time followed the course of the River Tame from Lady Bridge to a point in Lichfield Road just beyond the Bradfords, then skirted Staffordshire Moor round to the Leys, along Lud Lane, across Ludgate Railway Bridge, across to Salters Lane at its existing northern point but proceeding in the direction which Salters Lane must have formerly taken, to a point opposite Wigginton Road, turning south-east across the road junction and proceeding down Upper Gungate to the junction with Lower Gungate, along Albert Road and down Marmion Street and Mill Lane, following the site of Offa's ditch, then to Bolebridge, and along the River Anker but taking in a field called the Catcholme, and finally from the Anker at the point where the River Tame then joined it before flowing to the Castle Mills, up to the corner of George Street and Market Street, and then on the south side of Market Street to the Holloway. The Castle was outside the Borough, and the boundary in Market Street ran through the houses and shops on the south side and through the coffee-room of the Castle Hotel.

The Local Government Board did not favour the whole of the application of the Town Council, but made a Provisional Order extending the Borough to include the Castle and land near the river (then in the Parish of Tamworth Castle), and land lying between Marmion Street, Mill Lane and the Railway, the north part of Albert Road, and the east side of Upper Gungate and Ashby Road to a point nearly opposite the Spital Chapel, thus increasing the area from 200 to 285 acres, and the population from 4,888 to 6,614.

When the bill to confirm the Provisional Order was before Parliament, an attempt was made to transfer the Borough to

Warwickshire, an argument taking place as to whether the Act of 1888 had in fact automatically transferred the Warwickshire part to Staffordshire. It was finally considered that the Act had had that effect and that the area then proposed to be added to the Borough would likewise go into Staffordshire, and the Provisional Order was confirmed accordingly, the date of its operation being 1st November, 1890.

During the past half-century it has often been cited, wrongly, that Tamworth became a Staffordshire borough in 1890. The point is important in this respect : Tamworth became wholly a Staffordshire borough on 1st April, 1889, solely by virtue of the provisions of the Local Government Act, 1888, and not as a result of borough extension ; it could not help itself in the matter ; the extent of the populations in the two parts of the town was the deciding factor, and that meant Staffordshire. All that the Act confirming the Extension Order did was to extend the Borough boundary and to require that the extension so granted should also be in Staffordshire ; a similar provision was made when the Borough was extended in 1932.

Thirty years elapsed before the next application for extension was made. In 1919 the Council submitted to the Ministry of Health a scheme for a vast area to be included within the Borough ; it proposed to go beyond the area of Tamworth rural district, then in both counties, by including Polesworth as well. The scheme did not even reach the stage of a local inquiry ; it was completely rejected. In the following year, a reduced scheme was submitted. After a local inquiry lasting three days due to much opposition, a modified scheme was approved by the Ministry, involving the transfer of part of the parish of Bolehall and Glascote, and parts of Fazeley and Wigginton. Unfortunately, the opposition was carried to the parliamentary stage, and the bill submitted by the Ministry to confirm the scheme was rejected by a Committee of the House of Lords in May, 1922.

The next step to obtain an extension was taken in 1930. The Local Government Act, 1929, imposed a duty upon county councils to revise the boundaries of all districts within their areas at least every ten years. Tamworth, naturally, desired an extension on the Warwickshire side as well as in Staffordshire, but this could not be obtained under the Act as a county council could not make variations which would alter the boundary between two counties ; they could alter the boundaries of districts within their own county only. The Borough Council therefore decided to promote a bill in Parliament, the first in its long history as a borough, designed to secure an extension by the inclusion of certain parishes in Warwickshire, as well as parishes in Staffordshire. The proposal met with criticism from the other authorities, but eventually consultations took place which led to an agreement whereby part of the parish of Bolehall and Glascote in Warwickshire, and parts of the parishes of Fazeley and Wigginton in Staffordshire, were to be added to the Borough. The bill to confirm this was passed by a Committee of the House of Commons after a two-days' hearing and so, under the Tamworth Corporation Act, 1931, the Borough was extended to its present size on 1st April, 1932. The area of the Borough was thus increased from 285 to 2,678 acres, and the population from 8,032 to 11,711. The present boundary follows the Coventry canal from Amington Road on the east to a point near the River Tame on the west, then follows the river to Hopwas Bridge, and runs to the north of Coton Lane and Gillway, to the east of Brown's Lane and from thence across the River Anker to Amington Road.

Until this time, the Borough had never been divided into wards ; since 1835, when the members ceased to be self-elected, they had been elected by the whole of the burgesses. The enlargement of the area necessitated a variation in the size of the Council also, and therefore it was increased from four aldermen and twelve councillors to six and eighteen respectively. The ward system had to be introduced to facilitate voting at municipal elections, so the Borough was divided into three wards, these being given the names "Bolehall," "Castle" and "Leys."

The Borough as extended by the Act of 1931 remained in Staffordshire ; any proposal to transfer it from one county to the other would have resulted in increased opposition, with the risk of the bill being rejected completely as in 1922, although then for a different reason. It is now most unlikely that any further alteration in the county boundary will disturb the present arrangement, for the automatic settlement of 1889 seems to have firmly established the principle of Tamworth being a Staffordshire borough.

Chapter II

TAMWORTH CASTLE AND GROUNDS

THE ANGLO-SAXON CASTLE OF ETHELFLEDA, or such as remained of it after the destruction of the town by the Danes in 943, was granted by William the Conqueror, sometime after the Battle of Hastings (probably about 1070) to his Dispensator or Royal Steward, Robert de Marmion, one of his intimate followers who had accompanied him from Normandy.

Editha, the daughter of Edward the Elder and the sister of Athelstan, had established a convent in her aunt's castle or in its precincts. It is known that the convent was still in existence in 1010, for the will of Wulfric Spot, the ealdorman of Mercia, who founded Burton Abbey, referred to it. It is believed that one of the first steps taken by Marmion in taking over his new possession was to expel the nuns, who retired to a nunnery at Polesworth, which had been founded by King Egbert, whose daughter, another Editha, was the first Abbess. It is said that Marmion, who had a grant of lands at Polesworth, also ejected the nuns from the nunnery there, compelling them to seek refuge at Oldbury, near Atherstone. There is a legend which says that one night after Marmion had retired to bed, following an entertainment at the Castle, Editha appeared to him in a vision, dressed as a veiled nun, with a crozier in her hand. She chided him for his behaviour towards the nuns and, striking him with her crozier, prophesied that he would meet a terrible death unless he allowed them to return to their convent at Polesworth. Marmion, says the legend, vowed to carry out the request and kept his promise. The legend, however, is incorrect as to the date of the restoration of the nuns, for although they were expelled by the

27

first Marmion, it was the third baron who allowed them to return, in 1139 or 1140. The Public Library contains the original of a charter given by Sir Robert Marmion, the fourth baron, confirming his father's gift of Polesworth Abbey to the nuns. It reads : "To the prelates and ministers and all sons of the Holy Church of God, as well present as to come, and especially to Henry the Second King of the English and to Theobald Archbishop of Canterbury and to Walter Bishop of Chester, Robert Marmion son of Robert Marmion and Millicent, greeting in the Lord. Be it made known unto you all that I for my salvation and for the soul of my father and for those of my mother and my sister and all my ancestors have granted in perpetual alms to the nuns of Polisworda the gift of my father which he gave to them and as he gave it, which also by this my present charter I confirm, to wit the church of the same vill with the appurtenances of that church, and all the vill of Polisworda and all my lordship of Wavertune, in mills, in woods, in open ground, in waters, in meadows. All these let them have and hold freely and quietly . . "

It was the first Marmion who replaced Ethelfleda's wooden stockade on the mound by the Norman tower and keep we see to-day. Alongside it, to the east of the mound, he built the domestic quarters. The entrance was situated in the short passage which now leads from the Market Place. As late as the close of the eighteenth century the foundations of one of the round towers which formed the gateway could be seen. The Keep appears to have formed a circuit of the walls on the east side ; the site of the remainder of Marmion's Castle is taken up partly by the Castle grounds and partly by the yards and outbuildings of adjacent houses. A portion of the old walls can still be seen in the cellar of the Town Hall Vaults Inn which adjoins the present entrance to the Castle grounds. When Leland, the historian and antiquary, visited Tamworth in 1541 to report upon the College attached to the Parish Church, as part of his inspection of the monastries and religious houses at the time of their dissolution by Henry VIII, the buildings below the Keep were disappearing, for he recorded that "the base-court and great ward of the Castle is cleane decayed and the wall fallen downe, and therein be now but houses of office of noe notable buildinge. The donjon hill yet standeth and a great round tower of stone, wherein Mr. Ferrers dwelleth, and now repaireth it.''

Practically the only portion of the surrounding walls now in existence is the massive curtain wall which passes from near the spot where the tower of the entrance once stood to the Keep on the summit of the mound, and which has been very much lowered, so that it now forms a path, protected by modern side walls, to the Castle. This wall is ten feet thick, is believed to have been built by Ethelfleda, and is said to be the finest specimen of Anglo-Saxon herring-bone masonry in existence, although some experts claim that it is Norman.

The mound is a hundred feet high and forty-five feet in diameter. The fosse which ran round its base extended from the River Anker to Market Street and then down the Holloway to the River Tame. It appears to have been a dry ditch, about twenty feet wide. It is believed that there was a further defence between Church Street and Market Street, extending from Offa's ditch on the west of Aldergate to College Lane, and proceeding south along College Lane to the River Anker. In 1908 traces of this entrenchment were found in Silver Street and King Street, and at the point where College Lane joins George Street. There is in existence today, to the west of College Lane, a portion of an old wall which in all probability stood on the bank of the ditch, being on the line of the supposed entrenchment.

The Norman Keep and Tower contain walls nine feet thick in parts. Adjoining the tower is the Warder's House. From the courtyard a door in the wall of the Keep on the left leads up to the Watchman's lookout, and to the right of the Warder's House, underneath the Tower, is a dungeon thirteen feet square and eighteen feet high, with no windows or ventilation. It is thought that underneath lay another dungeon, now filled in.

The buildings within the Keep have been constructed at different periods. The northern part is the oldest and is probably the part occupied by the Ferrers mentioned by Leland in 1541. The portion on the south was built by Sir John Ferrers in the time of James I ; the entrance bears the arms of the Ferrers family, but the details are now much decayed. The kitchen on the west side was built by the Marquis Townshend some time before 1845 to replace rooms which had become dilapidated.

To the left of the entrance are private apartments occupied by the Castle Custodian. Near the kitchen is a very old well, about seventy feet deep, which passes through the mound to a level with the river. To the right of the entrance is the baronial Banqueting Hall, a magnificent room with a high-pitched roof, a large window on the east, and a large open fireplace on the west side. On the north wall of the hall there was formerly a fresco of the last battle between Sir Lancelot de Lake, one of King Arthur's knights, and Sir Tarquin, a valiant Saxon knight. The figures were of gigantic size, and were represented in tilting. The picture was whitewashed and finally obliterated in 1783. The battle to which it had reference, and for which there is no foundation in fact, was described in a ballad as having taken place in Lady Meadow, near Lady Bridge, about 519, Sir Tarquin being slain, his body flung into the river, and forty-four knights, prisoners in the Castle, released. For two years, from 1790, the Banqueting Hall was rented by the first Sir Robert Peel (then Mr. Peel, who had brought the cotton industry into the district from Lancashire) and was used as a blacksmith's forge in connection with a factory he had built in Lady Meadow, near Lady Bridge.

From the Banqueting Hall a staircase gives access to the south rooms, and another staircase to the rooms on the north side. The broad oak stairway on the west side of the hall leads to the State Drawing Room. At the top of these stairs is a window known as the "Minstrels' window"; it is believed that before Sir John Ferrers made alterations to the Banqueting Hall there existed a Minstrels' Gallery which was used when guests were entertained in the hall below.

The State Drawing Room is a fine apartment wainscoted throughout in oak. The frieze contains fifty-two panels bearing the arms of the Ferrers family and other lords of the Castle. The first panel, near the door leading to the Oak Room, bears the following inscription : "Here foloweth the coates of armes antiently borne in ye name of Ferrers, with an abstract of such howses and antient families as have since the Conquest been lynially descended from Henry de Ferriers, lord of Ferriers in Normandie, who came to England with William ye Conqueror, and tooke his first denomination from the said towne called Ferriers, lying in ye Dukedom of

Normandie.'' Three panels over the fireplace show the descent of James I and Sir John Ferrers from the same ancestor, David, King of Scots.

The room adjoining the State Drawing Room is now known as the Oak Room, and is also panelled throughout in dark oak. It contains further panels of the arms of the Ferrers. The notable feature of this room is the mantelpiece, with a panel containing the twelve principal quarterings of the Ferrers and the motto ''Only one.'' The figures of a man, woman and child are believed to be the likenesses of Sir John Ferrers and his wife and child. The surrounding panels bear mythological subjects, Jupiter, Prometheus and Adonis.

The other main rooms in the Castle are the Long Gallery, which formerly had partitions dividing it into four rooms, probably used as servants' bedrooms, and the State Dining Room, a fine apartment now used as a Picture Gallery. Adjoining this is the Royal Bedchamber, used by James I on his three visits to the Castle.

The Castle is now used as a museum, and contains many exhibits of local interest. Among them is a very fine collection of coins, many of which were issued from the Tamworth Mint, the earliest of these having been minted in the time of Athelstan. Other Tamworth coins in the Museum were made in the reigns of Eadwig (955-959), Eadgar (959-975), Ethelred II (979-1016), Edward the Confessor (1042-1066), William I, William II and Henry III. There are between three and four hundred coins, tokens and medals in the collection.

The first discovery of coins locally was in 1877, when excavations were being made in connection with the building of the Girls' Council School in Marmion Street. No less than 294 coins were then found in a leaden case in land known as the ''Hilly Field,'' near the corner of Albert Road and Marmion Street. The site was part of Offa's ditch. The coins were of the reigns of William I and II, thirty-three of them being those of the Tamworth Mint ; some of these Tamworth coins are now in the British Museum, and some in the local collection. The Council have at various times added to their coin collection by purchase.

Near the entrance to the Keep is a large stone, which formerly stood on Lady Bridge, then called ''the Bridge of Our Lady'' or "the Bridge of St. Mary," and which bore a pedestal with a statue or cross. It is believed that it bore the arms of the Marmions as well as those of Lord Basset of nearby Drayton and probably served as a boundary stone when the land on one side belonged to the Castle and on the other side to the Manor of Drayton.

The Castle Lodge, which is the main public entrance in the Holloway, was built by the Marquis Townshend in 1810, when the mound was planted and gardens were made.

Near the Holloway Lodge stands a statue of Ethelfleda and her nephew Athelstan. It was erected in 1913 to commemorate the thousandth anniversary of the building of the mound by the Lady of the Mercians, and was unveiled by the 11th Earl Ferrers.

On the eastern side of the Castle Grounds is an ancient well, which is believed to have been in existence since Saxon times. It certainly existed in 1276, for a record shows that one William Chelle was fined for placing an obstruction in the pathway to it. It is known as the well of St. Ruffin or St. Ruffianus. Wulfhere, a pagan King of Mercia, had two sons, Wulfade and Ruffin. Tradition says that one day Wulfade was hunting when he met St. Chad, who lived in a hermit's cell at Stowe, Lichfield, and had become Bishop of Mercia. St. Chad converted him and, later, Wulfade's brother Ruffin. Thereafter the brothers used to visit St. Chad to pray with him, until their father came upon them in their devotions and in his anger slew them both. Afterwards he repented. It is quite possible that Wulfhere came occasionally to Tamworth, as there may have been a palace here before that built by Offa, and so might have dedicated this well as a holy well in penitence for the murder of his son.

Turning now to the lords of the Castle, the first Marmion incurred the wrath of Henry I, and forfeited his possessions, dying soon afterwards, in 1101. It has been said that there is some doubt as to the identity of the first Marmion and his successor. Dugdale, in his *Antiquities of Warwickshire*, says that the first lord, known as Robert Dispensator or Robert the Steward, was Lord of Fontenay and Royal Champion, to whom the Conqueror gave Tamworth for his services at Hastings, and that the second baron, also named Robert, was his son. Palmer, on the other hand, in his *History of the Baronial Family of Marmion*, contends that Robert Dispensator and the Lord of Fontenay were different persons, and that the latter, said by him to be Sir Roger Marmion, became the second baron of Tamworth Castle as the successor to Robert Dispensator, that he was a kinsman, being a son-in-law, or grandson, but more probably son-in-law, and that his wife was the daughter and heiress of the Dispensator, and goes on further to say that the third baron was the son of Sir Roger. Be that as it may, the second baron received the forfeited estates of Robert Dispensator from the King, and occupied the Castle until his death in 1110. The king again came to the Midlands during the lifetime of the third baron, also named Robert. It was this Marmion who restored the nuns to their nunnery at Polesworth, from which they had been evicted by Robert Dispensator ; he supported King Stephen against the Empress Maud, daughter of Henry I, in her claim to the throne, and she in her victory confiscated the Castle in 1141 and gave it to Sir William de Beauchamp. Marmion met his death in an ignominious manner. In 1144 he had an affray with the Earl of Chester, a champion of Maud, and entered a priory at Coventry near the Earl's castle, expelling the monks and fortifying it by digging deep ditches, well covered with earth, as traps for the enemy in their approach. However, when he rode forth to meet the Earl's forces he fell into one of his own ditches and broke his thigh, whereupon a soldier standing by cut off his head. His body was taken to the restored nunnery at Polesworth, but the nuns could not give him burial in the consecrated ground there as he had been under the ban of the Church, and for many years his resting-place was in a corner of the nunnery orchard.

The fourth lord of the Castle, Sir Robert, son of the last-mentioned Marmion, had the Castle restored to him by King Stephen in 1153. He received a visit on 12th March, 1157, from Henry II, accompanied by the Archbishop of Canterbury and Thomas à Becket, then Lord Chancellor and subsequently a martyr. This baron spent much of his time in Normandy, where he had many possessions.

Upon the death of Sir Robert Marmion in 1185, his son, also named Robert, inherited the Castle. He was a student of the law rather than a warrior, although he is said to have been a gallant knight ; he was appointed by the king as an itinerant justice for the midland counties, and was also Sheriff of Worcestershire for four years. He served King Richard I and King John in wars in Normandy, but later sided with the barons who obtained Magna Carta from King John who, on 30th December, 1215, commanded his chamberlain to hasten with royal forces to Tamworth and raze the Castle to the ground, but whether or not any attempt was made to execute the order, the Castle was not destroyed.

Marmion the justiciary, who died in 1215, had two sons, both named Robert. The elder son having gone abroad soon after his father's death, the younger son obtained the custody of the Castle for some years. In 1220 his brother took his inheritance, and upon his death in 1243 the last of the male line of the Marmions and eighth lord, his son, Sir Philip Marmion, inherited the Castle. He became Sheriff of Warwick and Leicester, and in 1257 he entertained Henry III at the Castle. The Corporation archives contain a deed of grant to him by Henry III of the Manors of Tamworth and Wigginton in 1266. The records reveal complaints by the burgesses that he had interfered with their custom of electing their own bailiffs (or Mayors) every year, that he had required them to render service at his mills, that he had encroached on the King's highway, and that he sued two persons for breaking the gates of the Castle and carrying away goods worth £100. Towards the end of his life he founded the Hospital of St. James for the benefit of the Premonstratensian Order, but died before it was completed. This hospital was situate in Ashby Road. The chapel belonging to it, restored in 1914, still remains.

Sir Philip Marmion died in 1291, and his estates were then divided, Tamworth Castle being given to his eldest daughter Jane, and the Manor of Scrivelsby to the youngest daughter Joan. Upon the death of Lady Jane in 1294, the Castle passed to her niece, Joan Cromwell, who had married Sir Alexander de Freville. Among the civic records is a licence granted in 1323 by Edward II, who was entertained at the Castle two years later, allowing the Frevilles to assign the Castle to their son Baldwin. An inquisition taken in connection with the granting of this licence records that the Castle, with its appurtenances, was held of the King by the service of coming to the coronation, completely armed with royal arms of the livery of the King, sitting upon the principal royal war-horse, and opposing any person who should challenge the royal coronation, and that if none should offer opposition, the arms and the war-horse should revert to the royal use, but if any should oppose themselves, the arms, with the war-horse, should be taken for the use of the tenant of the Castle.   The Marmions had held a similar office under the dukes of Normandy as the tenure of their barony at Fontenay.   Sir Alexander performed the office of Royal Champion at the coronation of Edward III in 1327.   This, however, was the last occasion upon which the office was so performed by the possessor of Tamworth Castle, for the successors of Lady Joan Marmion, who, as stated, had succeeded to her father's estate at Scrivelsby, successfully claimed that the office belonged to that estate and not to the Castle at Tamworth.

The family of Freville originated in Cambridgeshire.   They had many possessions in the counties of Norfolk and Hereford.   Alexander de Freville was much engaged in the Scottish wars.   He died in 1328.   His wife survived him till 1339, and then their son, Sir Baldwin de Freville, held the Castle for three years.   His son Baldwin became possessor until 1375.   He served the Black Prince in the wars with France.   In 1348, during the plague, the inhabitants of Tamworth, resenting some offence, beseiged him in the castle and cut off supplies for some time.

Three other descendants, each named Sir Baldwin de Freville, inherited the Castle.   The third of these died in 1418, a minor and unmarried.   He left three sisters, and his possessions were divided among the co-heiresses, the Castle passing in 1423 to Sir Thomas Ferrers, who had married the eldest.

The Ferrers family traced their descent from Henry de Ferrers, who came to England with the Conqueror.   He obtained Tutbury Castle, as well as numerous possessions in fourteen counties.   His son was created Earl of Derby.   The eighth earl was attainted in 1264 and was disinherited by Parliament in 1266 for his share in the rebellion of the barons against Henry III.   From him and his brother William descended the two lines of the family of Ferrers, John, the son of the former, being created Baron Ferrers of Chartley in Staffordshire in 1299, while William, the son of the latter, was created Baron Ferrers of Groby in Leicestershire in 1297.

Sir Thomas Ferrers, who inherited the Castle by his marriage to Elizabeth Freville, was the son of the fifth Earl Ferrers of Groby.

The Castle remained in the possession of the Ferrers family until the seventeenth century. Three of them held the position of High Steward of Tamworth. Sir John Ferrers entertained James I at the Castle on 18th August, 1619, 21st August, 1621, and 19th August, 1624. The Parish Register contains the following entry : "1619, Aug. The 18th day James our noble Kinge and ye worthey Prince Charles came to Tamworth. The Kinge lodged at ye castell and ye prince at ye mothall"—the Moat House in Lichfield Street— "Mr. Thomas Ashley and Mr. John Sharp, then bailiffes, gave royal entertaynement."

During the Civil War, in the time of the Ferrers, the Castle was occupied in 1642 by the Royalists, and was a source of trouble to the forces of Cromwell in their endeavour to secure Lichfield. It was recorded by one of the officers of the Royalists that they "did keep their holy brethren from dulling their spirits with over much sleep in giving them several alarms, no rest nor respite night and day, with some particularised skirmishes." On 25th June, 1643, the Castle was captured by the Parliamentary Army after a siege lasting two days. The governorship of the Castle was given to Captain Waldive Willington of Hurley Hall, whose family could trace descent from Saxon times. The Parish Register records : "1643, June. Towarde the latter end of this month the towne and castell of Tamw. were taken from the enemy by the parliment's forces under the command of Coll. W. Purefoy." In the following year the Castle garrison successfully resisted an attack by two thousand Royalists from Lichfield. On 13th July, 1649, the Council of State ordered the Castle to be dismantled or destroyed but, as in the time of King John, the order was not carried out.

The last male descendant of the Groby family, John Ferrers, died in 1680, leaving a grand-daughter, Ann Ferrers, her father having been drowned in the River Trent in 1678. Ann Ferrers succeeded to the Castle, and in 1688 married Robert Shirley, the eldest son of Baron Ferrers of Chartley. The two branches of the Ferrers, Chartley and Groby, were thus reunited after an interval of more than four centuries. Baron Ferrers of Chartley obtained the title of Earl Ferrers, and that of Viscount Tamworth for the eldest son, in 1711.

Sir Robert Shirley and his wife died in 1697. Their son succeeded, and held the Castle until 1714, but died unmarried, and so it passed to his sister, Lady Elizabeth Shirley, who, in the following year, married James Compton, fifth earl of Northampton. Upon his death in 1754 his daughter, Lady Charlotte Compton, inherited the Castle. In 1751 she married the Hon. George Townshend, son of Viscount Townshend of Raynham in Norfolk. He was created Marquis Townshend in 1787. He died in 1807. His son, George Ferrars Townshend, carried out extensive repairs to the Castle, which had become neglected and dilapidated during the time of the Shirleys and the Comptons. He died in 1811, and in 1814 the Castle was sold under a decree of the Court of Chancery. It was purchased by Mr. John Robins, an eminent auctioneer of London, although seven years elapsed before he was able to take possession. He built the Market Street lodge, on the site of the old tower near the lane leading to the Market Place. Mr. Robins died in 1831. Owing to family disputes the Court of Chancery decided that his estates should be sold, and so, by public sale, the Castle came into the ownership, but not the occupation, of the Townshends again, Lord Charles Vere Ferrers Townshend, a son of the second Marquis Townshend, purchasing the property. He represented Tamworth in Parliament for many years. At his death in 1853 the Castle passed to his cousin John Townshend, and finally, when he died in 1863, to his son, John Villiers Stuart Townshend, the fifth marquis. He decided to dispose of the Castle by public auction.

The sale was held at the Town Hall on 8th June, 1897. Some time before, it was suggested that the Castle should be purchased by the Corporation. A public meeting was held, and it was decided to ask the Council, who had previously agreed that it was desirable that the Castle should be acquired for the town, to take steps to secure it in commemoration of Queen Victoria's Diamond Jubilee. At the sale, the first bid by the Town Clerk on behalf of the Corporation was £1,000. Two other bidders advanced the price to £2,500 and then a cry of "Let the ratepayers have it" resulted in a final and successful bid by the Corporation of £3,000. After the sale, the Council opened a subscription list, and the whole amount was eventually paid by public subscription.

So on 19th October, 1897, the Corporation completed the purchase of "All that castle of Tamworth, formerly situate in the

County of Warwick but now in the County of Stafford, with the offices, buildings, timber yard, court, bath, plantation and garden and all and singular the appurtenances thereto belonging, containing three acres two roods and sixteen perches now three acres and all that Honor of Tamworth Castle and all that Manor of Tamworth Castle and all that the manors, franchises, liberty and court of Stipershill with Wareton and Bolehall and Glascote in the County of Warwick and also the fishery of the old mouth of the River Tame as descending to Lady Bridge and the fishery from Lady Bridge unto Dunstall otherwise Tunstall, which said fisheries together with the site whereon two mills anciently stood in one house on the bank of the River Tame called the Lady Mills with the bays and banks into the old mouth in Fazeley are subject to an annual fee-farm rent to the Lord of the Manor of Drayton Bassett.''

Stipershill is between Polesworth and Warton ; here was held the courts of the lords of Tamworth Castle and all tenants of the estate were obliged to do their suit of service there. The fee-farm rent referred to was bought out by the Corporation in 1924, by the payment of £190 to Sir Robert Peel.

The Castle was formally opened on 22nd May, 1899, by the Earl of Dartmouth, Lord Lieutenant of Staffordshire, and was dedicated to the use of the public for ever. The day of the official opening was observed with great rejoicing in the Borough. The whole town kept holiday, entertainments were held in the Castle grounds, and at night the tower, battlements, terraces and grounds were illuminated with hundreds of fairy lights and lanterns. Over five thousand people visited the Castle during the day.

The Castle Mills formerly stood at the confluence of the Rivers Tame and Anker. They were held of the Crown by the lord of the Castle, and there the inhabitants of the town were required to have their corn ground, for in earlier times the grinding of corn at the lord's mill was one of the forms of suit and service. In the time of the Marmions the manorial mills stood on the same site ; during the lifetime of Philip Marmion, Ralph Basset, a descendant of the powerful family of Bassets of Drayton, Lords of the Manor of Drayton, erected mills at Bitterscote, the name given to the area in the vicinity of the ''Jolly Sailor'' Inn, with the purpose, no doubt, of annoying Philip Marmion in his control of the Castle Mill.

These mills were called the Lady Mills, and stood on the bank of the Tame at a place in Fazeley Road called Endall Ford, near a weir which existed until recent times. In those days the Manor of Drayton extended from Lady Bridge to Middleton Park. As a grant of land at Bitterscote had been made to a Benedictine Priory at Canwell, it is probable that these mills, together with Lady Meadow and Lady Bridge, derived their names from that association. The loyalty of the inhabitants to the local lords was divided, and they showed it even in grinding their corn. Philip Marmion, watching from his Castle tower, must have been considerably annoyed in seeing his tenants taking their corn to the rival mill, and, being a bold baron, he determined to stop it. Assembling a large band of Welshmen and outlaws in Tamworth, he attacked the mill at Bitterscote, and notwithstanding the number of Welshmen and others engaged by Ralph Basset, he broke open the doors, destroyed the mill pool and carried away the flour to his castle, and did damage to the amount of one hundred pounds. It was eventually decided "that because the counties of Stafford and Warwick had been disturbed by Welshmen and others congregated on behalf of the two parties, it is considered that they should find sufficient security not to introduce or maintain such men in future."

This resistance to the grinding of corn at the lord's mill persisted at times even up to the time of Queen Elizabeth I, for at that time many of the inhabitants, refusing to go to the Castle mill, erected small "querne mills" of their own at their houses. In 1589 the lord of the Castle, Humphrey Ferrers, obtained an injunction compelling the inhabitants to grind their corn at the "Queen's Cornmills."

The Castle and its grounds cover an area of about three acres. The lands formerly belonging to the Castle were extensive. There was the Castle Orchard, which lay to the west and north of Aldergate, and the Castle Liberty, which extended from the Castle precincts as far as Dosthill Hall, lying between the River Tame and the Kettlebrook and Dosthill roads ; this included land at Kettlebrook known as the Castle Park.

Considerable changes have taken place in the area to the south of the Castle. Until the latter part of the nineteenth century the River Tame divided at the weir near Fazeley Road, previously mentioned ; part ran near the road, as now, to Lady Bridge; but the main stream ran across the meadow in a north-easterly direction to join the River Anker to the east of the Castle Mill, near to the place where a concrete bridge now crosses the Anker. The present confluence of the two rivers, therefore, is not in the same position as formerly. After joining the Anker, part of the stream ran through the mill race, and the main part proceeded over the Castle Weir and ran to the south of the Castle Mill. There was no access to the land on the other side except through the mill.

In 1893 the Corporation and the Rural Sanitary Authority (which, in the following year, became Tamworth Rural District Council) jointly purchased the Castle Mill for the purpose of carrying out a scheme for the prevention of floods and also as part of a scheme for facilitating the drainage of the town and district. The Castle Mill was then described as a water mill, formerly described as three corn mills and one fulling mill, with the miller's house and outbuildings ; access was by a short road adjoining the Castle wall.

A joint committee of the two Authorities then carried out certain works. Obstructions in the Tame and Anker were removed, and a short branch of the Anker which enclosed a field known as the Catcholme was filled in. The Castle weir was removed, the mill race was stopped, and the mill pool between the mill and the present concrete bridge was filled in. It was decided to stop up the main course of the Tame so that the part then running direct to Lady Bridge would become the main stream ; in 1896 the joint committee allowed the Corporation to fill in part of the "trunk" of the Tame by using it as a tip for household refuse, and gave permission for the erection of a wooden bridge over the Anker to obtain access. This bridge remained until 1930, when it was replaced by the existing concrete bridge. The boundary between Staffordshire and Warwickshire had followed the main course of the Tame up to the Borough boundary, probably ever since the two counties were formed ; filling up the trunk meant that it no longer followed the river from Fazeley Road.

In 1900 the Corporation purchased the interest of the Rural District Council in the portion of land which was formerly the confluence of the Tame and the Anker (that is to say, the filled-in area near the existing concrete bridge) and also in the land near the old trunk of the Tame. Outbuildings to the east of the Castle Mill were demolished, and a small portion of land was added to the Castle Grounds so as to extend them to the new line of the river near the wooden bridge.

Then commenced a wise policy of extending and developing the possessions of the Corporation on the south side of the Anker, with the double object of disposing of household refuse and thus, by raising it above flood level, making it available for use as public pleasure grounds. The Corporation had long owned the Catcholme —there is no record of the purchase—it was described as "the common ground called the Catcharme" in a perambulation of boundaries in 1697. In 1906 land was purchased from the Trustees of Sir Robert Peel ; in the following year the interest of the Rural District Council in the Castle Mill was acquired, and further land was purchased from the Trustees of Sir Robert Peel in19 10. Further outbuildings of the Castle Mill were demolished in 1909 and the site was used to widen the path at the side of the embankment in the Castle Grounds.

Having acquired about fifteen acres of land, the Corporation in 1914 adopted a proposal to improve the Pleasure Grounds, including the replacement of the wooden bridge, which was becoming very ricketty and dangerous, by a concrete bridge. That scheme was only part of a programme which the Council had in mind. It received the approval of the Local Government Board, but unfortunately the outbreak of war and a restriction on public works caused it to be abandoned.

The Castle Mill was demolished in 1920, and the site was then used for a tennis court and ornamental gardens. Further land was purchased by the Corporation—Mill Meadow, Tamworth or Seckington Meadow, and Fazeley Meadow—until the total area of the Pleasure Grounds has now reached 60 acres.

For thirty years the Council continued the policy of developing the grounds by the tipping of household refuse. At first, the whole of the land was subject to flood ; gradually an area was raised above flood level sufficiently large to accommodate the town's cricket and football teams, but progress was slow, and in 1929 the Council decided to expedite the development, as it was considered that it would take a very long time to raise land adequate to meet the growing needs of the town for sport and recreation. Having obtained the approval of the Ministry of Health, following a local inquiry at which there was a certain amount of opposition, a bold scheme was carried out. It involved the raising of fourteen acres of land above flood level with 40,000 cubic yards of material obtained from colliery mounds in the district, and the construction of tennis courts, bowling green, children's playground, shelters, boat-house, refreshment pavilion and dressing-rooms, ornamental gardens and a concrete bridge to replace the rustic bridge. A new access to the grounds at Bolebridge was provided for the benefit of the residents of Bolehall and Kettlebrook. The newly-developed grounds, which were given the name of the Castle Pleasure Grounds to distinguish them from the enclosed grounds acquired with the Castle, were opened by the Lord Lieutenant of Staffordshire, the Earl of Harrowby, on 26th September, 1931.

In 1937 the Council completed a scheme for the construction of new Baths in the grounds. For half a century they had rented indoor Baths in Church Street during the summer months, but these had become out-of-date and totally inadequate for modern requirements. In view of the increasing popularity of open-air bathing, the impracticability of providing both indoor and open-air baths owing to the cost, and the suitability of the pleasure grounds, the Council decided in favour of open-air baths. The scheme consisted of a swimming pool, dressing accommodation, a café, and an area for sunbathing. From the commencement, the swimming pool became very popular.

The latest developments have been the construction of an open-air skating rink, and the erection of a bridge to give access to the grounds from Fazeley Road.

The pleasure grounds are frequently used for public events such as carnivals, galas and agricultural shows.

The Castle, which was scheduled by the Government as an ancient monument in 1915, and the extensive pleasure grounds, now attract visitors from many parts of the Midlands and the numbers increase every year. Forty thousand people paid the admission charge to see the Castle last year, and that number does not include the many parties of children allowed free admission for educational visits, or the thousands who, in the course of a year, benefit by their use of the public pleasure grounds. The burgesses who had the foresight to purchase the Castle in 1897 did better than they knew, for it can be said that it was the acquisition of this historic monument which has inspired later generations to carry out developments of which the town can well be proud ; few towns of the size of Tamworth can boast of a civic possession comparable to these fine pleasure grounds with such a picturesque background as the Castle.

Chapter III

TAMWORTH COURT ROLLS

THE ARCHIVES OF THE CORPORATION include about 250 rolls containing the proceedings of the manorial courts held in the Borough during a period of three centuries, commencing in 1288 and extending to the reign of Elizabeth I. It is possible from these to obtain glimpses of life in the town in those days. Palmer gives a few extracts from them in his *History of Tamworth*, but within the last two or three years, as a result of arrangements made by the Borough Council, the documents have been examined and summarised translations have been made, so that it is now possible to give extensive quotations from them for the first time.

The courts were the Portmanmoot Court, which met every third Monday, and the Court Leet or Court of View of Frankpledge, which met twice a year. The Portmanmoot Court dealt with claims for inheritance and settlement of property, cases of trespass and debt, and fined persons presented by the official testers for infringing the rules for bakers and brewers. The Court of View of Frankpledge supervised the frankpledges; it "viewed" the tithings to ensure that they were complete and that every freeman was enrolled in a tithing. It dealt with those who failed to keep the peace, took oaths of allegiance, appointed certain town officers, and made byelaws.

The Staffordshire and Warwickshire parts of the Borough had their own courts, presided over by the Bailiffs, and it would appear that they met on the same days. When the Borough received its charter of incorporation in 1560, uniting the town under one jurisdiction for municipal purposes, the grant included a court leet or View of Frankpledge, to meet twice a year, within one month after Easter and within one month after the feast of St. Michael the Archangel, to be held before the Bailiffs, and a Court of Record, formerly the Portmanmoot Court, to meet every third Monday and to be held before the Bailiffs, the High Steward and the Recorder. The Court of Record ceased to exist in 1792, and the Court Leet in 1876.

There are many references to the tithings. When burgages (a system of tenure in ancient boroughs whereby houses, and lands which were formerly the site of houses, were held of the lord by a certain rent) were taken up, the tenant was required to enter a tithing and pay an entrance fine, which for strangers was usually half-a-mark, the amount also demanded from strangers who entered the liberty by joining a tithing only. On 18th October, 1356, two men were assigned to a tithing and granted the liberty of the town without payment of a fine because their fathers and kinsmen were born in the town, while another man had to pay the usual fine because he was a stranger. On 24th April, 1489, John, son of William Irpe, was sworn into the liberty and paid 4d. because he was born in Tamworth after his father had been enfranchised. "Adam of Dedinton is received into the liberty of Tamworth and into a tithing as a free burgess" (23rd October, 1290) ; "John Brown has done fealty to the lord king and gives the Bailiffs 2s. for entry into the community and has been received into the tithing of John Elyot" (1st January, 1294) ; "John of Dileby is in mercy for receiving a certain boy outside a tithing" (11th June, 1294) ; "William of Billeye is received into a tithing and has made oath and if he conducts himself rebelliously let him be removed from the community" (25th November, 1303) ; "Richard de Hull is not in a tithing, nor is he fit to remain within the community of the town ; Henry le Suour has not been received into a tithing but he is allowed to remain in the town paying to the community a fixed certain rent as shall be agreed between them" (23rd May, 1306) ; "All those who have been received outside a tithing and who merchandize to be distrained to pay toll" (29th April, 1311) ; "Richard son of Robert Wele is aged twelve years and more and is not in a tithing" (15th May, 1326). A case of defiance of a tithing was dealt with on 13th November, 1290, when William of Schepeye was reported to be rebellious and opposed to the community of the town, he had broken his oath and had disclosed the "Counsels and secrets of the town" ; his tithing therefore rejected him on account of his rebellion and for not being submissive to jurisdiction. Two burgesses were fined on 15th May, 1357, for seeking another house outside the town against their oaths and against the custom of the town, and on 2nd November, 1358, it was ordered that all who dwelt outside the town for a year and a day, and who did not pay or give aid to their neighbours and the burgesses of Tamworth at all tallages, were to lose their liberty.

Two persons were expelled from the liberty of the town on 11th June, 1294, and it was ordered that anyone receiving the offenders would be liable to a fine, the harbouring of strangers and persons expelled being an offence. Henry le Taylor was amerced on 23rd May, 1295, for receiving John Grene after he had been renounced by the town. On 19th April, 1333, a burgess forfeited his rights because he had made orders and regulations to the harm of the community. Other cases of men being deprived of their rights as freemen were William of Norton and John Priour, a smith, who in October, 1388, were charged with bringing suits against Sir Ralph Basset to the prejudice of the town, and John, son of Thomas Walker, butcher, who had procured many indictments against his neighbours before the justices at Warwick (May, 1419).

The tithings wished to protect their members against fraud : "Roger Tooke bought a certain smith's instrument from a stranger deemed to be untrustworthy" (18th October, 1294). Usurers were not wanted : Henry of Sheile was fined on 23rd May, 1295, for being a usurer by lending silver and corn.

Welshmen came under a local ban in the fourteenth century. On 20th April, 1347, the court ordered that no one should receive Welshmen, under pain of half-a-mark, and a further byelaw made on 11th May, 1368, ordered that no men or women from Wales were to sell ale in Gumpigate (Lower Gungate) under pain of forfeiture of their ale each time. Welshmen had taken part in disturbances during the lifetime of Sir Philip Marmion, as related in a previous chapter, and there is every likelihood that the incursions of "the men from Wales" was resented in Tamworth as it was in other counties lying east of the Welsh border. In 1379 a petition was presented to Parliament by "the men of Staffordshire, Here-fordshire, Gloucestershire, Worcestershire and Shropshire" com-plaining of the way in which Welshmen had bought land in these counties and came in a warlike manner to kill, rob and ransom and take away beasts, goods and chattels and convey them to Wales, where the sheriffs and other officers of the king dare not exercise jurisdiction, so that these counties had been wasted and in a short time would be utterly ruined.

There was strict control of trading. In 1359 an order was made that no stranger dwelling outside the town should be in stallage, but that he should pay toll. This indicates a distinction between inhabitants who were either freemen or had paid to become stall-holders, and those from outside who paid toll. Nicholas Plow was fined for selling flesh without the Bailiffs' licence and before taking the oath (19th October, 1293) ; Ralf del Holt and Geoffrey Weneth sold 40 pigs to a stranger and paid toll for only 14 pigs (5th August, 1297) ; in June, 1310, butchers were warned against supplying goods to three shops held without the town's licence, and on 29th April, 1311, it was ordered that "all who are not in a tithing and who trade are to be distrained to pay toll" ; in October, 1324, William of Virley was distrained to appear before the Bailiffs to answer for concealing the avoidance of toll by strangers ; "Ordered by the twelve jurors that the Bailiffs take and cause to be levied the toll of the town from all common merchants as required by practice, custom and franchise and has been accustomed from ancient times, under penalty forfeited to the king and the com-munity of the town" (24th October, 1391).

Prices also were controlled. William Neel was fined on 10th November, 1298, for buying a cartload of salt in the market and then retailing it at 6d. a bushel when the price should have been 4d. or 5d. for the inhabitants ; Hugh of Bromkot (Bramcote ?) was fined for brewing ale at prices other than $\frac{3}{4}$d. or 1d. per gallon (1st Decem-ber, 1298) ; "Ordered that no brewer sell ale above $1\frac{1}{2}$d. a gallon, under pain of 12d." (15th May, 1357) ; in May, 1371, bakers were ordered to sell two or four loaves for 1d. according to weight, and brewers were ordered to sell new ale at $1\frac{1}{2}$d. a gallon and old ale at 2d.

In noting the fines imposed by the Court Leet, regard should be had to the value of money in those days. A common wage in the thirteenth and fourteenth centuries would be from threepence to fivepence a day, according to whether the labour was skilled or unskilled. A mark was two-thirds of a pound. As to the purchasing power of a penny, it would be difficult to compare the prices of commodities with those of the present day. It would be misleading, for instance, to think that ale would be cheap at 1½d. a gallon !

The burgesses were also protected against false weights and measures and other frauds. "It is presented by the tasters that the wife of Hugh the smith is in mercy for false bread once ; Ralf Toby for the same, twice ; Gregory Chella for short ale, twice ; Isabel at the Cross, for the same, once" (13th February, 1290) ; "Nicholas Alcus ordered to the pillory for false bread, three times now and twice before" (9th August, 1294) ; "William Knyth (amerced 6d.) and William Hendeman (pardoned) presented for putting straw into the flesh of calves for sale, thereby deceiving the purchaser" (8th May, 1332) ; "Ordered that all bread for sale unmarked be forfeited and that he who is found guilty be punished by the pillory" (2nd November, 1358).

We may think that food inspection is a modern health service, but centuries ago there were penalties for selling unfit food ; also for refusing to allow the official tasters to sample ale. Henry le Melemaker was fined on 29th May, 1290, for "not wanting the tasters to sample his ale." "William of Colleshull (Coleshill) is accustomed to sell flesh full of worms, putrid and diseased, and to keep much slaughtered flesh for three or four days without selling it, wherefore he is suspended from selling all flesh for a year and a day" (13th November, 1290). William seems to have been a regular offender for he appeared in both the Staffordshire and Warwickshire Courts on the same day, and was again before the court on 12th June, 1291, for keeping unsalted flesh four days, and yet again on 11th November, 1297, for selling flesh unlawfully in the market. "Nicholas, son of Alexander, sells flesh full of blood and uncleansed" (21st June, 1291) ; on 25th August, 1292, Ralph the skinner was fined for bad ale ; Nicholas Cek slaughtered a three-day-old calf which was not old enough according to the assize (29th April, 1311) ; "Ordered that the measures of Isolde Tooke be attached and examined against the standard because they are suspect'' (25th November, 1314) ; "All butchers are prohibited from keeping unsalted flesh beyond three days under pain of forfeiture of the flesh" (10th May, 1319) ; on 5th May, 1383, it was ordered "that no wine be sold before it is sampled and valued by the Bailiffs," "That no ale-wife sell ale except by measure sealed by the common seal, and that they do not sell before the mark has been affixed, nor after it has been removed." On 11th May, 1361, an order was made forbidding butchers to sell "old veal."

There are several references to the Saturday market in addition to those already mentioned. "John of Bollunhull (Bonehill) and six others amerced sums from 2d. to 6d. for having stalls in the market without licence of the community ; William le Meleward amerced 2d. for putting a table in the market without licence, also amerced 6d. for trading without licence" (22nd April, 1344) ; John Bally was sent to the tollbooth on 10th May, 1379, for buying and selling without paying toll ; an order that no one must sell grain in his house but must take it to the market, under penalty of 3s. 4d., was made on 27th October, 1438, and on 21st October, 1511, it was ordered that no grain be sold before the ringing of the market bell otherwise the grain would be forfeited. The number of licensed stallholders increased from 22 in 1422 to 40 in 1455.

"Forestalling" the market—selling goods before offering them for sale to all comers in the market or endeavouring to corner a commodity—was a common offence. "Margery Legister received a stranger who forestalls corn and other grain in the market ; William Neal, Ralph Neal and John of Hopwas forestall salt in the market to the harm of the community" (18th October, 1294) ; at the next court the same persons were also fined for forestalling salt in the market and selling at a dearer price. "Roger de Wychenor distrained for forestalling the market in selling herrings" (5th September, 1317). On 21st October, 1511, Eleanor Brome was warned not to forestall eggs and butter "at the end of the town" under a penalty of 12d. ; at the same court her husband was fined 4d. for forestalling the market with salt and warned that in future the penalty would be 40d. Another offence was "regrating"— buying goods wholesale so as to control supplies and to sell at retail prices. Three persons were fined on 21st October, 1438, for being "common regrators of grain, deceiving the king's people."

Bakers and butchers were subject to control, for many orders affected them. There seems to have been concern that the inhabitants should have sufficient food ; on 22nd May, 1419, it was ordered that all bakers must bake wholesome white bread and black bread regularly so that the town should be adequately fed, "under pain of 20s. or of giving up the said craft and changing to another" ; a further order was made on 2nd November, 1423, that if the town should be without bread, each baker must pay 40d., and on 9th November, 1428, it was ordered that if the town be without bread so that none was for sale, each baker must pay 8d., half going to the Bailiffs and half to the common chest, and the under-bailiffs were commanded to levy this without any indulgence. In May, 1446, butchers were ordered to sell their oxen and sheep at the Butchery (Church Street) during the whole week, and on Sundays meat must be sold until the eighth hour.

Executions were ordered by the court on 10th June, 1294, for the theft of three steers ; on 13th December, 1294, for housebreaking and stealing two dressed horse-skins, a tunic and a shirt ; on 16th April, 1332, for stealing a red cow, price 5s., and on 11th May and 7th December, 1332, for stealing pigs. It is said that the gallows stood at the junction of the Ashby, Wigginton and Comberford Roads, at the place now known as the Fountain.

The movement of labour was controlled by an order made on 5th May, 1383 ; "no labourer shall leave the town to work elsewhere in spring or autumn, nor any servant by day or by the week, under penalty of 40d." An Act passed after the Black Death in 1349 prohibited the movement of labourers to other districts in search of better wages, which were then fixed. Service to the lord of the manor is referred to in an entry for 5th November, 1366, when ten persons were fined for refusing to give their customary services in the autumn, and on the same day a burgess lost his liberty for not giving the customary services which he owed to the Bailiffs and the community.

"If anyone be a chatterer he shall have the cucking stool placed before his door and be put therein," said an order made on 23rd October, 1403. Lest it be thought that this order applied to males only it should be said that, in legal interpretations, words importing the masculine gender include females. Alice Barker and

Isabel Peynton were treated as common gossips to the disturbance
of the king's peace on 2nd May, 1441, and were required to reform
before the next court under penalty of 40d. ; we are not told whether
they complied with the order. Eavesdropping, like gossiping,
was not tolerated : William, the son of Edmay, was fined on 25th
May, 1311, for eavesdropping by night upon his neighbour's walls.
On 23rd March, 1332, a man was accused of standing by the wall of
a house "to listen to gossip, whereupon he was chased back to his
own house and battered."

The first reference to the town's watchmen occurs in the
proceedings of the court on 12th June, 1310, where it is recorded
that they were keeping watch as they were accustomed to do by
law, when they were attacked and beaten, and the hue and cry
was raised. On 12th May, 1366, it was ordered "by the community
of the town that each man or woman refusing to watch shall give
4d. to the Bailiffs on the morrow," and in the following November
Philip of Bedeford was fined "for refusing to watch with his neighbours according to the law of England." An order was made on
30th May, 1379, that if anyone was not prepared to watch and give
faithful vigilance from sunset to sunrise, as was the custom of the
town, upon order or summons of the Bailiffs, he would incur a fine
of 4d. for each refusal. Further orders were made on 30th May,
1390, requiring each burgess to send one able man to watch at
night, under pain of 40d. for each default, and forbidding men
constituting the watch to eavesdrop by the walls of their neighbours'
houses under a similar penalty, so this was a case of the watchers
being watched. In the following November it was ordered that no
man or woman should go after nightfall from one place to another
without carrying a light. Another order regulating the watchmen
was made on 29th May, 1391, prohibiting them from entering houses
to drink but they could stand outside by the door ! Also, if they
found anyone wandering about after a reasonable time they must
make an arrest and take the offender to the Bailiffs. On 4th May,
1411, it was ordered "that if any man goes into a tavern by day and
particularly by night with sword, staff, cudgels and billes to harm
against the peace, the Bailiffs and burgesses and the whole community of the town shall arrest him and put him into gaol and he
shall give 6s. 8d. to the Bailiffs and 6s. 8d. to the common chest,"

and a further order in 1422 prescribed a fine of 20s. if anyone interfered with an arrest by the king's watch. On 6th November, 1424, it was ordered that anyone found abroad after the ninth hour at night could be arrested and imprisoned until a pledge of £20 was found. There appears to have been a church watch as well as a town watch, for on 2nd October, 1329, there was a case dealing with an affray involving "the watch of the church of Tamworth and the watch of the town of Tamworth." Two persons were fined on 7th November, 1365, for refusing to watch at the church by summons of the Bailiffs.

It was the responsibility of the burgesses to "raise the hue and cry" against evil-doers, and so assist the course of justice, otherwise they could be regarded as aiding and abetting the offenders. The Court Leet proceedings contain many references to witnesses raising the hue and cry "justly"; on the other hand, giving the alarm unnecessarily was also an offence, as instanced by two persons being summoned on 7th November, 1289, for "unjustly raising the hue and cry." This responsibility of the townspeople is further illustrated by an order made on 18th October, 1435, that all must mutually rally to the aid of the bailiffs or under-bailiffs in executing the law, and that anyone refusing to do so must pay 20s., half to the common chest and half to the bailiffs.

The church is referred to in the court rolls on several occasions. The selling of grain "in the churchyard of St. Edith" was forbidden by order made on 1st May, 1425, (an Act passed in the reign of Edward I prohibited fairs or markets in churchyards for the honour of the church) ; "ordered that if any boy breaks the church windows his father shall pay 8d., 4d. to the Bailiffs and 4d. to the church" (14th May, 1425) ; arising out of disputes between the Bailiffs and the Vicars it was ordered on 9th May, 1429, that no person must invite any Vicar to his table under penalty of 6s. 8d. ; on 15th October, 1448, it was ordered that the Dean of the Church should ring the bell daily at the third hour, presumably to prepare and summon the faithful to early mass ; included in the proceedings for November, 1458, was the king's writ directing the Bailiffs that vicars, by law, could not be required to attend the View of Frankpledge ; on 17th December, 1443, a person was sued by "the keeper of the church lights" for stealing candles.

Orders were made on 23rd October, 1403, that anyone whose dog should be found outside his house after twilight must pay half-a-mark, and in November, 1423, "that no one lets pigs wander in the town, but that they be given into the custody of the swine-herd," and each tenant of a house must pay the swineherd one penny a quarter. A further order about pigs stipulated that the owners must keep them out of the market and the churchyard, otherwise there would be a penalty of 1d. for each pig (27th April, 1517). An order made on 5th May, 1421, prohibited the playing of "Tenys" or "Coyte" under a penalty of 40d. with the prospect of being committed to gaol, and on 18th October, 1457, a further order prohibited the playing of unlawful games such as "Kuteryng, quekkyng and hasedyng" after nine o'clock at night, and the harbouring or receiving of any person so playing. Another order made on 18th October, 1546, forbade any inhabitant to play unlawful games prohibited by statute and especially in the churchyard, and yet another, dated 15th October, 1516, prohibited all tenants from collecting money for ale or games in the church or town. On 27th April, 1517, it was ordered that no servants of any householder be out of their master's houses, nor play at knuckle-bones or dice after the hour of nine at night under a penalty of three days' imprisonment.

The ditch constructed by Offa was preserved by the Bailiffs, being let as gardens. Eleven burgesses appeared before the court in 1310 for encroachments with hedges ; in 1324 a person was fined for cutting down trees growing in the ditch ; thirty-one persons were fined on 8th May, 1332, for encroachments and it was ordered that the land taken must be restored ; on 18th October, 1356, eight persons were similarly fined and the hedges and enclosures ordered to be removed "this very day" ; and on 29th April, 1404, it was necessary to order "that if any tenant is occupying the king's dyke without paying rent, he shall appear at the next court to show his charter and to make fine ; if not, the Bailiffs and community may enter." On 22nd February, 1294, a messuage is described as extending from the highway by the Stone Cross (Colehill) up to the king's ditch (Marmion Street). The portion of the ditch which ran near the present Orchard Street was called the Walfurlong ; it is mentioned in an entry dated 10th November, 1488, when Maud

Irpe and her neighbours whose gardens adjoined the Walfurlong were ordered not to allow any animals to be bought or sold during fair time without paying toll.

An order made on 11th May, 1361, regulated the procedure with regard to the town chest : "It is ordered by the assent of the whole community that each Bailiff for the time being shall have custody of the keys of the common chest, and that when he leaves office he shall deliver the keys and rolls of the court to the Bailiffs at the time appointed, together with his charge, that six men of the county of Warwick and six men of the county of Stafford shall be at the showing and proving of the said chest in company with the aforesaid Bailiffs, and that one key shall be in the custody of the frankpledge of the county of Stafford and one key in the custody of the frankpledge of the county of Warwick." As stated in a previous chapter, the Borough was divided into two parts, owing to the county boundary running through the centre of the town, and each part had its own Bailiff or Mayor.

Expenses of the town's representatives "going before the King's Justices at Warwick upon the business of the town of Tamworth" were paid by a special tallage in May, 1306, when five men resisted the bailiffs collecting this tax. The Court must have been held in the vicinity of the Market Place according to the following entry for 16th March, 1299 : "It is granted by the whole community of Thameworth that Thomas of Copynhall may build a certain solar adjoining his house in Co. Warwick towards the highway opposite the pillory, so long as they are able to pass and ride there and hold their court at the will of the community." There is a reference in 1293 to a grant of land lying in "the lane below the bell," and in 1356 to a penalty of 20s. which if imposed should be put towards "the work of the bell," but where the bell or lane was, is unknown. Grants and exchanges of land are often recorded, sometimes with the measurements, as in 1290, when a plea was quashed because the defendant did not hold all the tenement claimed, a part in area 8 ft. by 16 ft. being held by Sir Philip Marmion, then lord of the Warwickshire part of the town. Strips of ground as narrow as 2 ft. exchanged hands, one, for example, being 200 ft. in length, and another 50 ft. In February, 1291, for the sum of 66s. 8d. paid in advance William Thelone took up "one place of land with the buildings thereon opposite the gate of the churchyard, containing 10 ft. in width and an equal length to that of the neighbours.'' Upon a grant of land in 1329 a burgess paid 6d. for entry, ''according to the custom of the manor.''

Legal procedure is referred to in several instances. When a husband refused to answer for his wife's misdemeanour by pleading that she had not been summoned to court, it was placed on record that ''the court says that it is the custom of this court for the husband to answer for his wife in a plea of trespass'' (17th November, 1292). A minor asked that his case should be postponed till he was of full age to answer, but the jury decided that he was twelve years and more and therefore able to plead (5th December, 1295). On 16th November, 1445, the jurors stated that it was the custom of the manor that anyone prosecuting another by a writ of the king in their court must appear in person unless he had licence from the Bailiffs and the court to appoint an attorney, and on 22nd October, 1454, it was stated that no one could be an attorney or have warrant of attorney unless accepted by the court, according to the custom of the town. In a case in the following October a person not having such warrant or licence from the Bailiffs was refused acceptance by the court.

The jurisdiction of the Court was sometimes questioned, as in 1293 in respect of land held of the Castle of Tamworth. On 7th September, 1444, certain property was alleged to be in ''Wyginton'' which was said to be a liberty of itself and an ancient demesne of the Crown ; at one time the Manors of Wigginton and the Staffordshire part of Tamworth formed one manor. It is interesting to note that in 1315 the bailiff of Sir Ralph Basset, lord of the manor of Drayton, claimed that a defendant living at Faresley (Fazeley) was his bondman and therefore not within the jurisdiction of the Tamworth court.

In 1358 a burgess was fined for impleading another in the Hundred Court before he had impleaded him in the court of Tamworth, and in the following year another burgess was fined for impleading his neighbours in the Hundred Court against the custom of the town before he had failed in law in the local court.

Claims for inheritance were dealt with by the court. It was recorded in 1334 that John of Pychford who held of the king one shop in the market place of Tamworth had died, and that John, his kinsman and heir, a chaplain, came and did fealty and paid 2d. for relief. Four years later, John the chaplain died and William of Whytacre claimed the shop as a perquisite of Sir Ralph Basset and asked for an inquiry by the court. The sister and heiress of John also claimed by her inheritance and likewise asked for an inquiry. The jurors decided that John the chaplain died seised of the shop by John his uncle and that it was not the perquisite of Sir Ralph Basset, that it was acquired by John the uncle after the time that he enfeoffed Sir Ralph of certain tenements in Tamworth, and they decided that the sister of John the chaplain was the next heir and she thereupon did fealty and gave 2d. for relief.

Enclosures of land were carefully watched by the court. In May, 1368, the frankpledges presented Thomas Ardene, knight, for enclosing a wood called "Elleford Lee" on the Staffordshire side and John de Clynton, knight, for enclosing "Periecroftezate" on the Warwickshire side, both of which should have remained open for all tenants. The first-mentioned was again reported in October, 1378, when the jurors said it was held separately although it used to be common land. In October, 1388, John Coton was fined for refusing to allow the town shepherd to pasture animals on the common pasture. The Abbot of Merevale was fined 6d. in 1411 for enclosing a part of common ground without licence. The court rolls contain a deed dated 25th March, 1286, giving the permission of the burgesses of the whole vill of Tamworth and the inhabitants of the manor of Wigginton for William le Sauvage, beloved clerk of Sir John Hastings, to enclose by dyke and hedge two acres of land in the common pasture. This was granted at the request of Sir John, then lord of the Staffordshire part of the town, witnessed by several knights and burgesses, and sealed with the seal of the community. This is also the first reference to a town seal. The seal is referred to again in a grant of land in "Le Swynesdich" in 1329.

In the later rolls the election of officers is recorded in detail. Thus on 21st October, 1505, those elected were two churchwardens, the constable, two collectors of the oxherd's stipend, two chamberlains, two wardens of Lady Bridge, and "keepers of the lights" at the altars of St. Mary, St. Nicholas and St. George in the Parish

Church. One of the official tasters was absent from the court on 3rd August, 1461, and the under-bailiff was ordered to warn the defaulter that he would be fined 3s. 4d. for each absence in future. Refusing to serve as a juror resulted in a burgess being fined 40d. on 27th October, 1461.

In recording the proceedings at the court on 21st October, 1550, the scribe lapsed into English, especially for the following orders given by the jurors : "Every man kepe ther gret dogges in ther howssys" under penalty of 4d. for each offence ; "No man shall receve no man in ther howssys att service tyme" under penalty of 3s. 4d.   On 28th April, 1551, William Wodde was fined for "keeping of servantes at ye sermonde tyme."

When the Borough was incorporated in 1560, the proceedings of the court became limited to judicial matters, as the charter of incorporation gave the corporate body the power to elect its own officers and to make byelaws and regulations for the better government of the town.

There are no records of the Court Leet for a period of two hundred years from the middle of the sixteenth century.   However, there is a continuous record, not in rolls but in book form, of the proceedings from 1751 to the last meeting in 1876.   During this period the Court Leet was combined with the Court Baron.   The latter Court is mentioned in the charter of 1560 ; it was a court ordained for the maintenance and service of the duties stipulated by the Lord of the Manor and for the purpose of determining actions of a personal nature where the debt or damage was under forty shillings.

The minute books of the Court Leet and Court Baron record the charge to the jury.   This commenced : "Gentlemen, This is a Court Leet and Court Baron.   In the Court Leet or View of Frankpledge you have power to enquire of and punish all offences against the Peace and determine matters of controversy between the King and Subject.   In the Court Baron you have power to enquire of and adjust all matters between Lord and Tenant.   First you are to enquire who they are that owe Suit and Service to this Court and those that have made default therein you have power to amerce.   In the next place you are to enquire if any person was presented at the last Court for any offence ; whether the same was reformed within the time limited in such presentment ; if so the penalty is to be set aside, if otherwise you must present accordingly that the penalty may be levied for the Lord's use.'' Then follows a list of the offences and matters to be investigated by the jurors : nuisances, ''a nuisance is that which is an annoyance or disturbance to many'' ; encroachments upon the King's highway by hedging, ditching, or enclosure ; the deposit of refuse or timber or other materials to cause obstructions on the highway ; failure to scour ditches or lop trees and bushes, thereby impairing the highway ; diversion of ancient ways or water courses ; the laying of any carrion or ''any stinking dirt'' in the highway by which ''the air is corrupted'' ; the obstruction of common streams ; ''eavesdroppers, such as listen under walls or windows or hear tales and report them amongst the neighbourhood'' ; ''all common barretors, scolds and other breakers of the Peace'' ; all riots, routs and unlawful assemblies ; all unlicensed alehouses, and failure to keep good order in those which were licensed ; all gaming houses, bawdy houses and ''other such lewd and disorderly places'' ; the failure of brewers, bakers, butchers and others to ''vend good and wholesome meat and drink fit for man's body'' ; and to enquire of the constables, surveyors of the highways and all other public officers that they had duly executed their respective offices. As to the latter, the Bailiffs themselves were sometimes presented in respect of matters which needed the attention of the corporate body.

The minute books contain a list of standard fines for the type of offences recorded in the rolls centuries before : Brewers not keeping a true assize of beer and ale, bakers selling bread under weight, chandlers for putting ''kitching stuff'' in their candles, and butchers for selling meat that was not good and wholesome, fourpence each ; country butchers and bakers attending the market, sixpence for the like offences ; allowing pigs to go into the churchyard or go loose in the streets, 3s. 4d. ; receiving or harbouring any stranger or setting any house or part of any house to any stranger or person from outside the manor without first giving security to save the town harmless from such persons and their families, £5 ; refusal to contribute to the repair of public wells and pumps by those who used them, 3s. 4d. Freeholders not appearing at court to do suit and service were fined sixpence each ; tenants, fourpence.

After the Borough received its Commission of the Peace in
1836, there were only five meetings of the Court Leet and Court
Baron, principally for the purpose of perambulating the boundaries,
as most of the work of the court leet was transferred to the justices,
and the Court Baron was superseded by the County Court.

CHAPTER IV

MUNICIPAL AND PARLIAMENTARY ELECTIONS

IT WAS NOT UNTIL 1563 that the Borough of Tamworth had direct representation in Parliament, but from that year until 1885, except for a period of five years from 1654 when Cromwell deprived the town of its direct representation, the Borough had two members. In 1832, as a result of the Reform Bill, the boundaries of the Parliamentary Borough were extended to include the ecclesiastical Parish of Tamworth, viz., Castle Liberty, Amington, Wigginton, Hopwas, Comberford, Syerscote, Fazeley, Wilnecote, and Bolehall and Glascote. When the boundaries of parliamentary constituencies were again revised in 1885, the Borough lost its direct representation, the Staffordshire part being included in the Lichfield Division and the Warwickshire part in the North Warwickshire Division. The name of the latter was changed in consequence of opposition by the Council in an endeavour to preserve the name of Tamworth in a parliamentary division because of the association of the town with parliamentary history ; on 7th May, 1885, the Council resolved "that the best thanks of the Mayor, Aldermen and Burgesses be given to Sir Robert Peel and to Messrs. Bass and Balfour, the Borough members, for the action taken by them in the House of Commons in securing that one of the parliamentary divisions of Warwickshire shall hereafter be called the Tamworth Division."

The next revision of parliamentary constituencies was in 1917. The Council in July of that year resolved to oppose a proposal to place the whole borough in the Lichfield Division (Tamworth having become wholly a Staffordshire Borough for municipal purposes on 1st April, 1899), and to support the retention of the old Warwickshire part of the Borough in the Tamworth Division of Warwickshire. They were not successful in the first aim, but they were able to persuade Parliament to continue to call the Tamworth Division in Warwickshire by that name instead of changing it to Coleshill or Sutton Coldfield. Upon the passing of the Representation of the People Act, 1918, the Borough continued, therefore, to give its name to a parliamentary division, although no part of the town came within it !

When the municipal boundaries were extended in 1932, the parliamentary boundary was not disturbed, so that the part then transferred from Warwickshire for municipal purposes remained in that county for parliamentary purposes, the Borough again being in two constituencies. That position obtained until the next revision of constituencies in 1949. It was to be expected that the town would again be placed in one constituency, obviously that of Lichfield, and that any attempt to preserve what many had considered to be an anomaly from 1918 to 1932 would be futile. The Borough did, however, object to its exclusion from recognition on the Staffordshire side, and was successful in obtaining an alteration in the name of the Lichfield Division to that of "Lichfield and Tamworth."

Notable men have represented Tamworth in Parliament, and several of them have made contributions to the municipal history of the Borough.

The first members (in 1563) were brothers, Michael and Robert Harcourt, who at one time lived at the Moat House. No doubt their election was due to a connection with the family of Devereux of Drayton. Walter Devereux, who was created Earl of Essex in 1572, owned the estate at Drayton which had once belonged to the ancient and powerful family of Basset. For a long period after acquiring the right of direct representation in Parliament, Tamworth came under the influence of the successive owners of the Drayton estate.

Edward Devereux, brother of the Queen's favourite, the second Earl of Essex, who procured the town's charter of 1588, was one of the representatives from 1588 to 1592. With him was Robert Wright, who later was one of the conspirators in the Gunpowder Plot.

Sir John Ferrers, who owned the Castle when James I paid three visits there, was one of the members from 1603 to 1621. He was also Sheriff of Warwickshire and High Steward of Tamworth.

The names of two members are linked with the Civil War : Strode, a Cromwellian, who was one of the five members of the House of Commons whom Charles I attempted to arrest, and Stanhope, a Royalist, who was killed in battle.

Sir Thomas Thynne, who also lived at Drayton Manor, became one of the members in 1679, although he held office for only a year. It was he who gave to the Borough, following his election, its seal bearing the fleur-de-lis, diapered with small flowers and containing the inscription "Sig.Burgi de Tamworth in Comitat Warwic et Staf"—seal of the Borough of Tamworth in the Counties of Warwick and Stafford. In 1951, when a new seal was made, the Borough Council decided to retain the original design and inscription as a reminder of the former association with Warwickshire, although the Borough ceased to be in that county in 1889. Does the fact that Warwick appears first in the inscription signify a possibility that in 1679 the Borough attached more importance to Warwickshire than Staffordshire, bearing in mind that whenever the county boundary has been under consideration, from 1888 onwards, it has been considered by some that Tamworth ought to be a Warwickshire borough ? For the town went wholly into Staffordshire on 1st April, 1889, only because at that time the greater population of the two parts, although the difference was very slight, was in the Staffordshire portion, and the Local Government Act of 1888 enacted that any borough then in two counties should henceforth be situate in the county in which the largest population lived on the day appointed.

Sir Thomas Thynne was appointed High Steward of the Borough in 1681. In the following year he was created Viscount Weymouth. This family owned property in the Borough for several generations. A descendant was created Marquess of Bath in 1789, the eldest son then taking the title Viscount Weymouth.

Thomas Guy represented Tamworth in Parliament from 1695 to 1707. He was born in Southwark, London, in 1644 or 1645. His mother was Anne Vaughton, who was a native of Tamworth. She returned to Tamworth after the death of her husband. Thomas, who was then about eight years old, was sent to Tamworth Grammar School. At the age of 16 he went to London, and was apprenticed for eight years to a bookseller in Cheapside. He became very successful in business as a bookseller in a little shop at the corner of a street opposite the Mansion House. His early success was due to the great demand for English Bibles, for the printing of which he secured a contract with the University of Oxford. He became a freeman of the Stationers' Company and a freeman of the City of London, which he also served as an Alderman.

Guy maintained a close association with Tamworth. He was successful in being elected to Parliament on six occasions, but in 1707 the local electors changed their politics and he was defeated. He never forgave the town for this, even when he was asked to stand for election again. He refused, saying that Tamworth had been ungrateful to him, considering what he had done for the town. He had, in fact, in addition to the gift of the Town Hall, erected alms-houses in Lower Gungate, and on 20th July, 1693, the bailiffs and capital burgesses, in giving him permission to build a wall fronting the street there, referred to him in their minutes as "our incomparable benefactor." His will, made shortly before his death in 1724, excluded the inhabitants of the Borough from participating in the benefits of his almshouses, restricting them to people living in Wilnecote, Glascote, Bolehall, Amington, Wigginton and Hop-was. This restriction still applies in relation to the boundaries of the Borough as they existed in his day. He used his wealth in assisting St. Thomas's Hospital in Lambeth, and in erecting the hospital in Southwark which still bears his name. The almshouses he built in Tamworth were replaced by new ones in 1913.

In 1790, Robert Peel was returned unopposed as one of the Borough members. He had previously bought the Drayton estate from Lord Weymouth. Introducing the cotton industry into the district from his factories at Bury in Lancashire, he erected mills at Fazeley and Bonehill, rented the Castle Mill, and built a factory in Lady Meadow. Already prosperous when he came to Tamworth, he acquired still more wealth and gradually purchased much land and many properties in the town and district until he became the principal land-owner. He was created a baronet in 1800. His second son, William Yates Peel, also sat as Borough member with his father from 1818 until 1820, when the latter retired. The son, who became a Privy Counsellor and occupied several posts in the Government during his career, continued to represent Tamworth until 1830, when his more famous elder brother took his place as one of the Borough members, but the two brothers both sat as the local representatives for two years from 1835.

Sir Robert Peel in 1820 established a school in a yard (which became known as Old School Yard) on the west side of the Parish Church, for one hundred poor boys who, in addition to free education, received a shilling loaf each week. The school continued to be maintained by his son, the Prime Minister, who erected a new school in Lichfield Street, near New Street, in 1837. This building also proving to be inadequate, a new building known as the Peel School, now a factory, was erected on the opposite side of the street in 1850, just before Sir Robert's death. The school continued until it became unnecessary by the provision of public elementary schools under the Education Act of 1870.

When the first Sir Robert Peel died in 1830, he was succeeded by the son who was destined to become Tamworth's most famous representative. The second baronet was born at Bury in 1788. He was educated at Harrow and Oxford, and was returned to Parliament as an Irish member at the early age of twenty-one. He soon came to office, being appointed Under-Secretary of State for the colonies in 1810, and from 1812 to 1818 he was Secretary for Ireland. Becoming Home Secretary in 1822, he held that office with distinction. He abolished the death penalty for a large number of offences, and introduced humanitarian reforms in the criminal law. The work for which he is most remembered in his service as Home Secretary was the creation of the Metropolitan Police Force in 1829, which laid the foundations of the present police system, his name being perpetuated in the word "bobby." At one period his brother William served him at the Home Office as his Under-Secretary of State. Seeking election at Tamworth in 1830 following his father's death, his address to the electors, written from Whitehall, stated that whatever leisure he could thereafter spare from the occupations of office, and from the necessity of attending upon His Majesty, would be devoted to residence in the neighbourhood and to the cultivation of those feelings of reciprocal confidence and goodwill which had so long subsisted between the inhabitants of Tamworth and members of his family.

Sir Robert Peel accepted office as Prime Minister in 1834. It was to the electors of the Borough of Tamworth that he made, in the election campaign early in 1835, his memorable address known as the Tamworth Manifesto, setting out his proposals which ultimately brought a new outlook to his party. He declared his readiness to adopt the spirit of the Parliamentary Reform Bill, which had been promoted by the previous government and had by then become law, saying that it constituted a new era and that he recognised the need to review institutions, civil and ecclesiastical, to correct abuses and to redress grievances. As to local government, he reminded the burgesses of Tamworth that he had been a member of the Committee of the House of Commons which had first dealt with the question of municipal reform before the appointment of the Commission referred to in the first chapter of this book, and he promised a full and unprejudiced consideration of any recommendations which the Commissioners might make. His party, however, although improving its position at the poll, did not secure a majority, and in the following April the new government was defeated, so that Sir Robert acted as Prime Minister for only five months. When the Municipal Reform Bill came before Parliament later in the year, he supported it, and opposed amendments proposed by the House of Lords which were designed to allow aldermen a tenure of office for life and to permit freemen to retain their rights.

Sir Robert became Prime Minister a second time in 1841. After a few years of office, came the question of the repeal of the Corn Laws. Peel, who had been opposed to the repeal, changed his opinion, convinced that the state of the country at the time demanded such a course. He always had the courage to alter his views whenever he came to feel that the progress of events justified or required it. He knew that his altered convictions on the Corn Laws would lead to dissension, but nevertheless he pursued the course which his conscience told him was the right one. He achieved a victory ; the Corn Laws were repealed, but only a few days later he was defeated on an Irish bill and resigned. His closing words in his last speech in Parliament before laying down his office are worth recording again : "It may be that I shall leave a name sometimes remembered with expressions of goodwill in the abodes of those whose lot it is to labour, and to earn their daily bread by the sweat of their brow, when they shall recruit their strength with abundant and untaxed food, the sweeter because it is no longer leavened by a sense of injustice.''

Four years afterwards he was thrown from his horse, and died three days later, on 2nd July, 1850. He was buried in Drayton Parish Church, in accordance with his wishes, although Queen Victoria had asked for a State funeral and burial in Westminster Abbey. The Tamworth Town Council attended the funeral. A service in commemoration of his death was held in Tamworth Market Place on Sunday afternoon, 2nd July, 1950, attended by the Council and the member of Parliament for the Lichfield and Tamworth Division, Mr. Julian Snow. By a coincidence the name of the presiding Mayor was Councillor W. A. Peel.

A statue of Sir Robert Peel was erected in the Market Place in 1852, bearing the following inscription : ''The Right Honourable Sir Robert Peel, Bart., born February 5th, 1788, elected in the year 1830 member of Parliament for Tamworth, which town he continued to represent until his death, July 2nd, 1850.'' The minutes of the Corporation record the unveiling ceremony thus : ''23rd July, 1852. The Council having met at the Town Hall in their robes, accompanied by the clergy of the town, adjourned to the Market Place where a raised platform was prepared for them and where they were met by the principal inhabitants of the town and neighbourhood. Sir Charles Mansfield Clarke, as the chairman of the Testimonial Committee, and in the names of the subscribers, after an eloquent speech, addressed the Mayor, saying, 'Sir, I give into your custody and that of the Corporation of Tamworth the statue of the late Sir Robert Peel and request that it might be preserved and protected as the statue of an erudite scholar, an eloquent man, and a profound statesman.' The Mayor accepted the trust and engaged on his own behalf and that of the Corporation to carry out the injunctions of the honourable baronet.'' One week later, it was ''resolved unanimously that the Council confirm the proceedings of the 23rd July last relative to the statue of the late Right Honourable Sir Robert Peel, Bart., and with feelings of pride accept the trust confided to them on that occasion, and undertake to preserve and protect the statue in remembrance of their late distinguished and lamented representative.''

Queen Adelaide, widow of William IV, visited Drayton Manor in 1839, and Queen Victoria, accompanied by Prince Albert, visited her Prime Minister there in 1843. On both occasions the Tamworth Town Council gave a civic welcome to the royal visitors in their passage through the Borough.

Sir Robert Peel was elected High Steward of the Borough in 1830. In his letter thanking the Bailiffs and Capital Burgesses, he said, ''To preside over a corporate body of great antiquity and unblemished character, to fill a post which has been occupied through a long succession of years by men of great eminence, cannot fail to be gratifying to those feelings which are inspired by an honourable ambition. But this appointment has a higher value in my estimation, than that which it derives from such consideration. It is the uninfluenced and unanimous indication of the esteem and friendship of those who have been known to me from my earliest youth, whose interests and welfare are concurrent with my own and whose good will I have every motive and every wish to conciliate.'' He took the oath of office of High Steward at a special meeting of the Bailiffs and Capital Burgesses held on Christmas Day, 1830. He was the last to occupy that office, for it became obsolete on 1st January, 1836, when the Municipal Reform Bill came into force. In 1838 it was proposed that the office of High Steward should be revived, and Sir Robert was invited to accept the office again, but he declined, giving his reasons in a letter dated 15th October, 1838, which is preserved amongst the Civic Records. He said the law (as it had been amended by the Act of 1835) had made the Mayor the first officer of the corporate body, that the appointment of High Steward would be merely honorary, although complimentary and valuable on that account, but that if such an office should be revived, then the formality, even if it was only a formality, of obtaining the consent of the Crown must surely be revived also. He continued : ''Would it be quite decorous in me to re-assume, say, in an address to the Crown, the extinguished title of High Steward of Tamworth, without having gone through the respectful ceremony which formerly was necessary, and having applied for the consent of the Crown ? But by applying for that consent, I may receive this answer, that the Mayor was the Chief Officer, that the law recognised no such appointment as that of High Steward, that the Secretary of State should not therefore advise the Crown to place the Mayor in an inferior position to that which the law assigned to him. It appears to me that this would not be an irrational answer, and at the same time, not an agreeable one, particularly to a devout Secretary of State.'' The decision was characteristic of him, for had not he himself been ''a devout Secretary of State'' ?

His eldest son, Robert, who became the third baronet, took his father's place as one of the members for Tamworth. He was then in the diplomatic service, having commenced such a career six years previously when his father, then Prime Minister, sent him as British Attaché to Madrid. Sir Robert's tenure of a Tamworth seat lasted for thirty years, during which time he served as a Lord of the Admiralty and as Chief Secretary for Ireland. It was during his lifetime that the financial troubles of the Peel family began. In the course of fifty years from 1871, when part of the fine collection of pictures was sold, the Manor estate, which once had an area of over ten thousand acres, decreased in size with the necessity to find money, until the remainder was sold in 1926, when the fine mansion which had been built upon the site of the old hall by the second baronet was demolished. One result of the various sales, however, was that the many possessions of the Peels in Tamworth, as in the surrounding district, came into the hands of others and allowed more scope for individual ownership and development, for the extent of the land and houses thus released was considerable.

A member of another branch of the Peel family sat in Parliament as one of the Tamworth members for seven years between 1863 and 1872. He was Mr. John Peel, a Manchester merchant, who came to live at Middleton Hall, upon his retirement from business. He was very popular in the town and district.

The right of sending two members to Parliament had the effect, for much of the time over a period lasting nearly two hundred years, of creating two separate and distinct interests or parties in the town, Drayton Manor and Tamworth Castle, and the two seats were regarded as belonging to those parties. The Castle interest became prominent again in 1812, when Lord Charles Townshend became

The Mayoral Chain, 1890

the second member.   He was the younger son of the second Marquis Townshend.   His brother owned the Castle, although not living there, but two years later the Castle was sold, and about thirty years afterwards it was bought by Lord Charles.   At the election in 1818 there was disagreement between the first Sir Robert Peel and Lord Charles Townshend, the latter accusing Sir Robert of going back upon an arrangement that no members of the Peel family would oppose one of the Townshend family, for William Yates Peel, the second son of the baronet, stood as a candidate, supported by his father.   Lord Townshend was defeated, but was re-elected in 1820 when Sir Robert Peel retired.   He continued as a Tamworth member until 1835.

John Townshend, a cousin of Lord Charles Townshend, sat as a Tamworth member from 1847 until 1853, when he became Marquis Townshend and owner of the Castle upon the death of Lord Charles.   His son, John Villiers Stuart Townshend, from whom the Corporation purchased the Castle in 1897, was elected in succession to his father, and held the seat until 1863, when he became the fifth Marquis.

When the Borough lost its direct Parliamentary representation in 1885, the first member for the North Warwickshire Division, which changed its name to the Tamworth Division, was Mr. Philip Albert Muntz.   It was he who gave a Mayoral chain and badge to the Borough in 1890, in commemoration of his performing the opening ceremony of the Assembly Rooms in the previous year. The chain is made of 18 carat gold and contains seven shields : (1) The arms of the County of Warwick ; (2) the arms of the Tudors, Queen Elizabeth I having given a charter of incorporation ;   (3) the arms of the Diocese of Lichfield, Tamworth being in that diocese since the days of St. Chad ;   (4) a Danish helmet with raven's wings, being the Danish emblem, Tamworth having suffered during the Danish invasions but being restored during the peaceful reign of King Canute ;   (5) the arms of the Plantagenet kings, the Borough having received a visit from Henry II and Letters Patent from Edward II, Edward III and Richard II ;   (6) the arms of the County of Stafford, and (7) a central shield containing the arms of the donor.   The circular badge at the foot of the chain bears a richly engraved fleur-de-lis, which has been the badge of the Borough since the days of Queen Elizabeth, with the inscription contained in the Borough Seal. The chain also contains facsimiles of the two maces first used in 1560.

A badge for the use of the Mayoress was obtained by private subscriptions in 1939, and one for the use of the Deputy-Mayor was purchased out of the rates in 1957. Both have the design of the Borough Seal.

It should be placed on record here that, unfortunately, the Borough has no grant of a coat of arms. This was revealed by an enquiry made at the College of Arms in 1936. The College stated that in the Heralds' Visitation of Warwick and Stafford in 1683 there appeared a representation of the Seal, a fleur-de-lis ornately diapered within a circlet inscribed "Sig: Burgi de Tamworth in Comitat: Warwic: et Staff:" with a note appended "engraven round the edge of the seal—ex dono Thomas Thynne de Maneiro de Drayton armigeri anno. dom. 1679." As it had sometimes been assumed that the Borough possessed arms consisting of the fleur-de-lis on a shield with mermaids as supporters, the College was asked whether there was any record of this. The College, confirming that no arms had ever been registered there for the Borough of Tamworth, said that the seal referred to by the Heralds appeared to have been placed upon a shield but there was no authority for the supporters (the mermaids) and that in 1568 such arms had been granted to the Borough of Boston in Lincolnshire. The Borough Council were invited by the College to submit an application for a grant of arms (such arms could not, of course, be similar to the alleged design in view of the grant to Boston) but the Council were of the opinion that the fees involved, £136. 10s. 0d., made it too expensive a matter, and so the Borough has to be content with a crest or badge, which is a replica of the seal.

It was stated at the beginning of this chapter that Tamworth did not commence to elect members to Parliament until 1563. In 1265, when Simon de Montfort, in his fight for the principle of the representation of the people in the national assembly which then became known as Parliament, caused writs to be issued requiring the sheriffs of the counties to return two knights from each shire, two citizens from each city and two burgesses from each borough, Tamworth did not participate. Palmer says that as the town was in the power of one of the most faithful adherents to the king, Sir Philip Marmion, that may have been the reason for its exclusion. In spite of efforts by Parliament to prevent false returns by sheriffs, many boroughs continued to be excluded, and Tamworth appears to have been one of them. As the town first had its direct representation three years after receiving its charter of incorporation, it is possible that that event caused action to be taken by the county sheriff.

Having obtained the right of election, the power was exercised by the Bailiffs and Capital Burgesses. This was objected to at a later date, for in 1639 eighty-seven burgesses submitted a petition to the House of Commons complaining that the householders had no voice in the election of the members to serve for the town in Parliament, quoting as an example an election made in the previous March when, "without any notice at all given of the time and place for election," the Bailiffs and Capital Burgesses had proceeded to choose the local representatives, and alleging that the right of the burgesses was "thereby much intrenched upon." The petitioners were unsuccessful. In 1670, the matter was again raised, John Ferrers, an unsuccessful candidate, petitioning against the election of his opponent. A committee of the House of Commons decided that the power of election belonged exclusively to the corporate body. Nine years later, however, it was decided upon another petition that the right of election belonged to those inhabitants paying local rates and not receiving alms, and also to those persons who had freehold premises in the borough, whether they were residents or not. In 1722 it was decided that non-resident freeholders were to be excluded from voting. It would seem, therefore, that the practice of the Bailiffs in allowing votes for the election of parliamentary representatives had varied, which is not to be wondered at, seeing that on one occasion one of the Bailiffs was the steward of a candidate. From the narrow circle of the local governing body the voting went to the other extreme of admitting non-residents to the vote, and finally, to the inhabitants paying local rates as decided upon the petition in 1722.

The first half of the nineteenth century was a period when election literature, in the form of handbills, posters and squibs, kept Tamworth printers working at full speed. The Castle Museum and the Public Library contain an enormous quantity of such documents. The town seems to have possessed a number of local poets, ever ready to pour out doggerel revealing a very low standard of taste and lack of tolerance. No wonder that Tamworth became a noted place at election times, when feelings ran very high, often ending in election petitions. A whole book could be written about these diatribes.

Those were the days when bribery and corruption held a prominent place in election proceedings. The town records include several documents throwing light upon the procedure in those days. A report by the agent of the Right Honourable George Townshend in 1760 revealed that he "found the friends of the present Members in some hurry and confusion as many of the Burgesses besides your Tenants would give no answer till they heard what part you would take but upon producing your letter it gave them great spirits and immediately came to a resolution to canvas the town and ordered Billets to all the publick houses for a treat of Liquor of half-a-crown a man ; Mr. Luttrell (the opponent) sent billets to all the publick houses where he could expect to gain any friends, to provide Dinners and Liquor for his voters for Wednesday ; we on behalf of the present Members ordered the same for their friends, to such (Publick) Houses as were in the interest of the present Members and who had refused Mr. Luttrell's billets, which gave them great spirits ; on Wednesday in the evening the owners of the Houses who had accepted Mr. Luttrell's Billets began to murmur very much that they had provided Dinners and so few came to eat them."

A memorandum (undated) of favours promised by Lord Townshend "to the voters at Tamworth" included the following : "To get Richard Knight, brother to Tom Wilkins' wife, a labourer's place in the Tower—he is a butcher ; To remove Mr. Benj. Vaughton from the Irish to the English Establishment ; Old Robert Tubb an outpensioner of Chelsea to have the King's letter ; Mr. Shirley promised to procure William Arnold, the younger, Chandler and Soap Boiler—an Exciseman's place or a place in the Customs ; Samuel Freeman, brother to Thomas and Wm. Freeman, to have a Side waiter's place or something in the Ordnance that will be bread for him ; To send Mrs. Wilson some Madeira ; To send some Turnep seed to Mr. Roby and a man to hoe Turneps in the

Summer ; N.B.—Lord Townshend to consider which of his Tenants he would have turned out ; Whether Moggs and Goddin should have land.''

Contentment after an election is shown in the following letter to Lord Townshend from his agent in 1765 : ''Mr. Thurlow's election is ended very peacefully, no other candidate was proposed, and about fifty of your Lordship's friends voted for him. It was thought best that your Lordship's friends should be invited to breakfast at the Castle on the Hill, and have some cold roast beef and ale. A great number came and they were very well pleased.''

An agreement dated 6th March, 1761, made between the Right Hon. George Townshend (the Castle interest) and Simon Luttrell (a candidate at the 1761 election) set forth a plan that as soon as the election was over ''the Castle'' and Mr. Luttrell should join their interests and at a joint and equal expense endeavour ''to bring in two for Tamworth and each party to name one,'' but in case they should find it prudent to agree for one only, then the nomination was to alternate between the Castle and Mr. Luttrell, and that in case they should judge proper, ''to compromise with Lord Weymouth (the Drayton Manor interest) for one and one ; the working of the colliery at Wincote (Wilnecote) ; the restoring the Corporation to the old usage of dividing the Aldermen (the capital burgesses of the Borough) equally between the Castle and Drayton Manor, and the settling the Town Clerk's and all other places dependent upon the Corporation equally between the Castle and Drayton Manor, shall be made preliminaries.''

Another document bearing the heading ''Sketch of a proposal for an agreement at Tamworth, Dec., 1763'' proposed : ''Lord Weymouth to have two members, and to fill up in case of vacancies for the remainder of this Parliament, at the end of which the Castle Interest to name one, and Mr. Luttrell, as his friend, to be named as the other member on the part of Lord Weymouth, with the privilege of the Castle Interest and Mr. Luttrell to fill up respectively upon vacancies during the next seven years, if that Parliament continues so long, after that Lord Weymouth and the Castle Interest to have one and one ; the Corporation to be restored so that the Weymouth and Castle Interest may have a constant equal balance in it.''

In a further document, dated 29th October, 1765, it was agreed between Lord Townshend and Lord Weymouth "that Lord Weymouth will use his interest to fill up one half of the Corporation with Lord Townshend's friends as soon as can be done with security and convenience to the united interest."

The "interest" of Drayton Manor and the Castle in the constitution of the Corporation is again revealed in a letter to Lord Townshend from his agent, written in 1766, in which he reported : "Today the Bishop of Lichfield has been here on a confirmation visit. The town treated his Lordship with a very handsome dinner. The Bishop enquired very kindly after your Lordship and drank your health at dinner, which went round as given in a bumper. Old Moggs observed that he thought your Lordship and Lord Weymouth ought now always to be drank together. He was seconded by Baillie Howe"—one of the two Mayors of the Borough—"which occasioned a smile from the Bishop and a pretty hearty laugh thro' the company. His Lordship with the clergy and some of the Corporation are just now come down to drink tea at Mr. Willington's and while it is getting ready I write this to your Lordship. Mr. Russ thinks it still too early to sound the Corporation as to the vacancies. He seems to have no doubt of a majority if necessary to push matters ; but as it is equal if done during Mr. Willington's baillieship, he wishes to postpone the proposition for some little time. The last step he says was rather contrary to the inclination of several of the Corporation, methods may be fallen upon. He thinks to unite them entirely, but patience is requisite to effect it. Next Thursday's entertainment may probably give me an opportunity, with the assistance of Mr. Willington's Strong Beer, to discover the real sentiments of those that are suspected and then we shall know how to proceed."

Mr. Willington was an aspirant for the office of Bailiff. On 28th July, four days before the annual election of the two Bailiffs, Lord Townshend received the report that "those proposed for Baillies are Mr. Willington and John Blood. Mr. Willington seems to have no great opinion of his colleague but says he will certainly stand in case he is chosen as he thinks it very necessary for your Lordship's interest, and on that account will do his utmost to get elected. This point gained, it is then proposed to fill up the vacancies"—namely, vacancies among the capital burgesses, or councillors—"for it seems the consent of one of the Baillies is absolutely necessary in the appointing of the Council, and there is a doubt of obtaining this from the present set." Mr. Willington and Mr. Blood were duly elected Bailiffs at the annual meeting on 1st August, 1766.

Mr. Willington wrote to Lord Townshend on 9th August, 1766, as follows :—"My scheme was to have invited the Corporation to supper whilst Mr. Lees is here, but as your Lordship is so kind to insist upon my taking Venison and intimating a Dinner, I intend to invite the whole body to dine with me on Thursday next. I had a Buck from . . . forest last Thursday, which I sent to . . . , and they all desired compliments and thanks to your Lordship. The rest of the Venison shall be distributed as soon as it can conveniently be got. Many of the Ale-house people have occasion for money, and all your Lordship's proportion will go in supplying their immediate necessitys, so that I cannot help paying them, but it is done so privately and without ostentation that it cannot give the least offence to Lord W. or the most delicate person in the world."

A document drawn up in 1765 gives "a list of the Corporation" and sets out the respective interests as follows :—"Lord High Steward : Lord Weymouth. Recorder : Mr. Munday ; Town Clerk, Mr. Oakes : alternate from each interest. Members belonging to Lord Weymouth's interest : John Vaughton and Walter Howe (Bailiffs), Nathaniel Crosland, clothier ; Thos. Butler, white smith under great obligation to the Castle interest ; James Oliver, linen draper ; Thomas Hinckes and Thomas Nicholls, clothiers ; Saml. Crosland, woolstapler ; John Osborne, formerly a clothier but now infirm and reduced ; Simon Collins, clergyman and school-master of Tamworth ; William Weston, carrier ; Saml. Prinsep, apothecary ; Joseph Alport, formerly a clothier but now reduced and under-steward to L.W. ; Edward Ball and John Blood, mercers. Members belonging to Lord Townshend's interest : Saml. Pipe, clergyman ; James Oldershaw, apothecary ; Benjamen Price, clerk ; John Willington, gentleman. Infirm and cannot attend the Corporation business : John Lattemer, clothier ; Peter Godwin, blacksmith. Reside out of the Corporation and ought to be disfranchised : Edward Wolferstan, gentleman ; Edward Woodcock, yeoman." The document bears the endorsement : "Lord Weymouth has now sixteen friends resident in the Corporation. Lord Townshend has only four, who are capable of acting. May not Edward Wolferstan and Edward Woodcock be voted out, and John Lattemer and Peter Godwin be prevailed upon to resign and Lord Townshend name four in their stead, and also fill up the two present vacancyes, and then his Lordship will have ten friends in the Corporation and then to fill up the vacancys as they happen till his number be equal with Lord Weymouth, after that when a vacancy happens the same to be filled up by Lord Townhend, or Lord Weymouth, which happens to have a friend, make the vacancy. For the future, one Bailiff to be named by Lord Townshend's friends and the other by Lord Weymouth."

In those days the governing body of the town was a "close corporation," the members being self-elected. No wonder someone tried to "pull the strings" ; no wonder that at last, by the Municipal Corporations Act, 1835, the power of electing the local governing body was given to the burgesses, for the day of municipal reform had arrived.

The Act of 1835 fixed the hours of voting at municipal elections as 9 a.m. to 4 p.m. It would appear that the Mayor counted the votes (the secret ballot did not begin until 1872) at various times during the day, for at the election in 1869 printed handbills, which must have been hot from the press, were issued showing the state of the poll. The following table shows how the poll progressed :—

	10 a.m.	12 noon	2 p.m.	2.45 p.m.	4 p.m.
Hill	104	187	270	298	320 (4)
Bailey	104	185	270	300	325 (1)
Hooper	103	187	271	301	322 (2)
Chater	100	176	268	297	321 (3)
Aitken	72	135	206	226	264 (7)
Stemson ...	68	131	198	218	252 (8)
Groom ...	72	134	205	224	265 (6)
Hamel	71	129	199	219	267 (5)

The candidates elected were Bailey, Hooper, Chater and Hill. There must have been unusual excitement at this election. The

Mayor issued a printed poster addressed to "the municipal electors of the Borough of Tamworth." He said : "Ladies and Gentlemen: A paper, dated Oct. 20, 1869, and bearing the signatures of Messrs. Hill, Bailey, Hooper and Chater, has been brought under my notice. In it, I find the statements that 'the Council is deeply, ruinously in debt,' and also that '£1,000 at least is needed to free the Borough Treasurer from the calls upon him.' I feel it incumbent upon me to assure you that both these statements are totally untrue, and I append the Balance Sheets, and Statement of Accounts both of the Town Council and Local Board, for your inspection. I have the honor to be, Ladies and Gentlemen, Your obedient Servant, F. Ruffe, Mayor."

The Mayor's statement could not have satisfied the electors, as the candidates he mentioned were successful at the poll ! It may be, of course, that he published the progress of the poll in the hope that those who had not yet voted would rally to his support when they saw that the critics were winning.

CHAPTER V

THE CORPORATION AND THE PARISH CHURCH

IT IS NATURAL that the Parish Church should take its place in this municipal history, for the present noble edifice and its predecessors have played their part in shaping the civic as well as the ordinary life of this ancient town.

When King Offa celebrated some of the Christian festivals at his royal palace at Tamworth in the eighth century and also signed royal documents in the presence of bishops and other ecclesiastical dignitaries, there must have been a church of some kind in existence, for it is unlikely that the capital of Mercia had no building in which to worship. Indeed, it is most probable that the first church was in existence much earlier than that, for the settlement of the missionary-minded St. Chad at Stow, Lichfield, in the seventh century, would undoubtedly lead to the establishment of a church in a town only seven miles from the newly-created See.

Whatever kind of church existed, it stood upon the present site. The destruction of the town by the Danes in 874 included the church also, and the second building was erected when the town was rebuilt in the time of Ethelfleda. This church was the scene of a royal ceremony on 30th January, 925. Athelstan, nephew of Ethelfleda and successor to Edward the Elder, entered into a peace treaty with the Danish king Sihtric of Northumbria, and gave his sister Editha to him in marriage, Sihtric undertaking to accept the Christian faith. Within a few months after the marriage, Sihtric broke the treaty and relapsed into paganism, and was slain in a battle in the following year. Editha retired to the convent at Polesworth which had been founded by King Egbert and of which his daughter Editha had been the first Abbess in the previous century. Here King Edward's daughter served her novitiate, and later established a convent in the precincts of Tamworth Castle, where she spent the rest of her life in acts of devotion and almsgiving. She would share the sufferings of the burgesses when the Danes again visited the town in 943, after the death of her brother Athelstan, and Tamworth was destroyed a second time, the church being ruined in the process. Editha, sometime after her death in 960, was canonized in remembrance of her piety and holy life, and was made the patron saint of Tamworth Church, the date of her burial, July 15th (now July 26th with the alteration of the calendar) being fixed as the date of her patronal festival.

It is said that King Edgar, the nephew of St. Editha, refounded the church about 963, and made it a collegiate church ; it is probable that the canonization of his deceased aunt took place at that time. There seems to be some doubt about the date of the rebuilding of this third church. At the time of the Reformation, Commissioners appointed by Henry VIII reported in 1545 that Tamworth Church and its College were founded by King Edgar, but Leland, the historian, who visited the town in 1541 to report on the church and its college, recorded that the church had a dean and six prebendaries, but he could not ascertain who had founded the college, and that he had been told by some that it was founded before the Conquest, and by others that it was of the foundation of Marmion, that the latter was most likely to be true, and that the King was the patron of the College. The six prebends were Amington, Syerscote, Wilnecote, Coton, Bonehill, and Wigginton with Comberford, all within the ecclesiastical Parish of Tamworth. Commissioners appointed by Edward VI reported in 1545 that the college of Tamworth was founded by King Edgar to find six prebendaries to sing divine service within the collegiate and parish church of Tamworth.

Whether or not Robert de Marmion, who built the Castle, also rebuilt the Church, one of his sons, William de Marmion, was reputed to be Dean.

An inquisition taken in 1291 following the death of Sir Philip Marmion, the last of the male line, recorded : "The church of Tamworth was in the donation of Sir Philip Marmyon." The patronage of the church after the Marmions, despite the claims of the Frevilles who followed them, returned to the Crown until it was sold during the reign of Queen Elizabeth I.

On 23rd May, 1345, the town and the church were destroyed by a big fire. The inhabitants must have suffered greatly, for three months afterwards royal authority was given for the payment of reduced taxes. Four years later disease and famine caused further hardship. No wonder, therefore, that the rebuilding of the church took many years, and was a courageous task led by the Dean, Baldwin de Witney. Out of the ruins of the damaged church arose the fourth and present structure, begun about 1350 and completed about 1369.

The Deanery lay between the east end of the Church and Lower Gungate, the main entrance being in that street. It was burnt down in another fire which destroyed part of the town in 1559, and only two portions of the walls now remain. In 1470 one of the Bailiffs gave a house and garden in College Lane (then called Cocket's Lane) for the priests of the college. College Lane School now stands on the site. A portion of the wall of the College House is still visible in the school yard and at the rear of Colehill.

Henry VI gave assistance to the Dean and Canons in 1445 by establishing a perpetual chantry in the church, to which a chaplain was to be appointed to celebrate mass daily, receiving towards his support the fee-farm rent of £5. 16s. 0d. per annum paid to the Crown by the Bailiffs and commonalty for the Warwickshire portion of the town.

At the dissolution of the monasteries the College was dissolved and much of the property of the church was sold. It was then decreed that the church should continue as the Parish Church, and that there should be a Preacher and two other Ministers, who should have as their residence the building in College Lane occupied by the late Vicars of the college.

It was originally intended that the Church Tower should have an exceedingly high central spire, but the plan was abandoned when it was discovered that subsidence had taken place, and four corner pinnacles were erected instead. The base of the abandoned spire can be seen rising to a height of ten feet above the battlements.

A notable and unusual feature in the Church is the double

spiral staircase in the tower. It is the only one in existence in the country ; the only other known double staircase is in the Château of Chambord, near Tours in France. It is possible for persons to ascend and descend the two stairs without meeting, one entrance being in the churchyard and the other in the tower. It is likely that this arrangement had a purpose, for the nightly watch of the church as well as the town watch, and the watchmen would thus be able to ascend the tower from the outside.

The monuments in the church include the tombs of Baldwin de Witney, Sir John Ferrers, Lady Dorothy Ferrers, Lady Joan Freville, and Sir Baldwin Freville and his wife. There are several stained glass windows of note, including the "Angels of Creation" windows by Sir Edward Burne-Jones, and the "Marmion" windows designed by Ford Madox Brown and executed by William Morris. The latter windows depict the marriage of Editha and Sihtric in the presence of Athelstan and Ella, Bishop of Lichfield ; Editha as the Abbess of her nunnery in Tamworth Castle ; and William the Conqueror presenting the Castle to Marmion, with the Marmion legend of Editha striking the baron with her crozier. These windows were given by Mr. F. Willington in 1873. He claimed descent from Athelstan and Marmion, and an ancestor of his was governor of Tamworth Castle for a time during the Civil War.

Some of the meetings of the Court Leet were held in the church. An order made by the assent of the frankpledges on 29th April, 1372, directed them "to attend on Monday every week as it comes round at the church of Tamworth for the mass called 'le brothur messe' to order and amend the constitutions made by them at their great Court, and that they shall not omit to do this under pain of 3s. 4d. each." "As it comes round" no doubt meant every third Monday when the court met. The "brother mass" was celebrated every morning in the Parish Church for the benefit of the members of the Guild of St. George. The guild was one of the religious and social guilds which existed at that time for the encouragement of religious practices, the exercise of works of charity, and the support of schools and schoolmasters. The members met for religious purposes in the chapel on the north side of the church dedicated to St. George, their patron saint, and the guild hall stood, it is believed, on the site of the present almshouses in Lower Gungate.

In the Court Leet rolls for 1384 there is a reference to Schoolmaster's Lane lying on the Staffordshire side of the town leading from Gungate to the churchyard. This indicates that there was an educational institution in Tamworth at that period, probably assisted by the guild. A century and a half later the chaplaincy of the guild was united to the mastership of the free school of the town, which was later re-founded by Queen Elizabeth. At the Reformation the guilds were abolished, and their funds and property were taken by the Crown. The guild at Tamworth was dissolved and its funds confiscated.

The commission of Edward VI, as already stated, ordained that Tamworth Church should remain as a parish church and that there should be a preacher or vicar, and two assistant curates. Queen Elizabeth in 1581 granted the advowson and right of patronage to two persons named Edmund Downing and Peter Ashton, who disposed of their rights, which were soon afterwards re-sold to Thomas Repington, whose ancestors came from Lincolnshire and had settled at Amington Hall, near the Ashby Road. Complications arose when the Queen duplicated the grant by giving to the Corporation, in her second charter of 1588, the right to nominate and appoint "a fit and erudite Preacher of the Word of God to serve in the Church of Tamworth and also two Ministers or Curates to serve in the same Church from time to time for ever, by the assent and allowances of the Chief Steward of the Borough." This grant was made to the Bailiffs and Capital Burgesses along with the power to appoint the master of the Grammar School. Frequently the person appointed as master was also appointed Vicar. The double grant of the right to appoint the Vicar led to a disagreement between the Corporation and the Repingtons which lasted for nearly two hundred years, although open warfare was avoided until near the end of that period.

The minutes of the Corporation record the appointments made by them under the charter, and other decisions relating thereto. In 1694, having appointed the Reverend Samuel Collins as Vicar, they ordered, so as to give him a civic welcome, "that seven strikes of malt be brewed and laid in the College for the use of our Minister, Mr. Saml. Collins, at his coming to the town, to be paid for out of the Town Box," and they appointed Mr. Jno. Davis, Junr., "to see to this.'' In the following year they must have been pleased with the services of the new Vicar, for they decided, "for the better encouragement of our worthy Minister, there be paid to him by the Chamberlain five pounds yearly out of the Town stock," and "that the Bailiffs with such of the Capital Burgesses as they shall think fit do attend on Mr. Repington when he is pleased to go to the Bishop and give his Lordship thanks for his great care of us, in the present Minister, and humbly desire that he will be pleased when anything shall offer that is in his power, that his Lordship would be mindful of him, whose means in this place is very small.''

The dispute with the Repingtons came to a head in 1758, although several years were still to elapse before it was finally settled. On March 13th of that year, apprehending that Mr. Repington intended "to deprive the Corporation of their rights to present or appoint a Minister to the Church of Tamworth, under pretence of a prior right," the Bailiffs and Capital Burgesses decided that a caveat should be entered in the Bishop's Court to prevent any presentation being entered under the pretended claim of Mr. Repington in order that the right might be legally settled at the death of their incumbent, the Rev. Robert Wilson. When Mr. Wilson died, the Corporation lost no time in taking action. On the very day after his death, the Bailiffs and Capital Burgesses met, and appointed the Reverend Simon Collins. One month later, having been strengthened in the meantime by an opinion obtained from Counsel that they had a clear and undoubted right to nominate and appoint the Vicars, and "it being apprehended Mr. Repington will pursue his pretended claim, and presuming that this suit will for ever hereafter establish the just claim of the Corporation to the elections and nominations," they ordered that Mr. Collins should be assisted out of the Chamberlain's Box towards defraying the expenses of defending any action taken against him.

Mr. Repington appointed William Sawrey, but Mr. Collins refused to surrender his appointment ; legal action was taken against the Corporation and Mr. Collins. The case was heard at Stafford Assizes in 1761 ; Mr. Repington was successful, and Mr. Collins was compelled to resign.

Notwithstanding this decision, the dispute continued. On 27th October, 1761, the Bailiffs and Capital Burgesses, considering that it might be necessary that other proceedings in law and equity should be commenced and prosecuted in order to assert the right of the Corporation, authorised Mr. Collins to make use of the name of the Corporation in any proceedings which might be necessary, and also authorised him to prosecute or defend any proceedings in the name and on behalf of the Corporation.

The Reverend W. Sawrey filed a bill in the Court of Exchequer against Mr. Collins and the Corporation, and on 26th January, 1764, the Bailiffs and Capital Burgesses instructed their attorney not to proceed any further in the matter, "the Corporation having determined to expend no more money in or about the premises." However, three months later it was agreed that there was a necessity for an answer to be put in on behalf of the Corporation to the bill which had been filed against them, and in case Mr. Collins could not afford to bear the expense, authority was given to the Bailiffs to take Counsel's opinion upon "the most safe and speedy method of putting an end to the suit," and they were authorised to take such action as Counsel might advise.

On 17th January, 1765, faced with a bill for legal costs since 1759 amounting to £265. 7s. 2d., of which £151. 7s. 2d. remained owing, and recording that the money in the hands of the Chamberlains was "greatly insufficient" to pay the bill, it was decided that the sum of £120 should be raised by mortgaging three houses in Market Street belonging to the Corporation.

The plea and answer of the Corporation to the bill presented by Mr. Sawrey in the Court of Exchequer was sealed at meetings held in 1766 and 1767 ; this led to further costs of £132. 0s. 9½d., towards which they paid £100 but the minutes do not state whether the balance was paid. No doubt the Bailiffs and Capital Burgesses were heartily sick of the whole business. It would appear that Mr. Collins went a little further by lodging an appeal to the House of Lords, but it was withdrawn in 1771, and he must have paid his own costs, for there is no further record of the Corporation *versus* the Repingtons in the matter of the nomination of Vicars of Tamworth.

Another matter affecting the Corporation and the Parish Church was St. Editha's Fair. This fair was probably held in Anglo-Saxon times, and later, the church having been dedicated to her, the fair also was named after her ; it may be that the fair began on the date on which her canonization was celebrated, by reason of the crowds which would congregate on those annual occasions. Because of the fruit brought to it, the fair became known as the Cherry Fair. In an inquisition taken in 1266 it was stated that the Dean and Canons of the church received the issues of the fair. At the Reformation, when ecclesiastical property was taken by the Crown, this fair also was included, and Queen Elizabeth granted it to the Corporation in her second charter of 1588. Thomas Repington and others claimed the profits of the fair, as having been sold to them with the church and the prebends, but the Bailiffs and Capital Burgesses were successful in obtaining an injunction in the Court of Chancery in 1589, authorising them to receive the profits of the fair until it should be otherwise ordered, on the ground that there was an express grant of the fair in their charter whereas there was no reference to the fair in the sale of the church property. In an action in the Court of Exchequer in 1592, however, it was held that the fair belonged to certain prebendaries of the dissolved College of Tamworth, which they held by letters patent granted in 1582; the Bailiffs made their claim under their charter, but "proved no right." There does not appear to be any later record in this matter, but as the Corporation now own the Cherry Fair it must be assumed that they maintained their claim under the second charter of incorporation, granted by Charles II in 1663, when the fair was re-granted.

After the Reformation the ringing of church bells often fulfilled a secular as well as an ecclesiastical purpose. In many towns and villages Ave bells, rung in the morning and evening, indicated to the people at a time when clocks and watches were few, the hours of rising and retirement, and at the same time served as a call to say their morning and evening prayers. The evening bell was also a reminder of the time when the curfew was rung. In Tamworth, the Borough Council decided in March, 1871, following the receipt of a letter from the churchwardens, to accept responsibility for the annual payment of the sum of eight pounds for ringing the bell at six o'clock in the morning and eight o'clock in the evening, probably because the Council considered that the ringing of the bell at those times served a public purpose as well as continuing what must have been an old custom. The bell-ringer must have soon neglected his duties, for two months later it was resolved that a fine of one shilling be imposed on the ringer whenever he failed to ring the bell. A correspondent writing to the *Tamworth Weekly News* in 1864, complaining that the curfew bell did not then ring, said that since the death of the curfew bell people had been seen repeatedly in the streets after eight o'clock in the evening, and on Saturday nights as late as midnight, as if they did not know "what's o'clock"; that the morning bell told them when to get up and go to work, and the evening bell when to leave off and go to bed; and on Sundays, in consideration of their having worked hard all the week and drunk hard overnight the morning bell kindly allowed them to lie in bed two hours longer, till eight o'clock, in order to allow nature to recover itself from the effects of their usual labour and overtime, and on Sundays also, as a reward for their having gone to church and back, tolerably sober once at least during the day, the evening bell intimated, by not ringing at all, that they might remain up all night.

In 1885 the Council resolved that the ringing of the curfew bell be discontinued, and they reduced the annual payment of five pounds for the six o'clock morning bell only. In 1933, in a desire to reduce civic expenditure, this payment was also discontinued. At that time the bell was rung at 7 a.m.

The Parish Churchyard has been extended at various times. Originally the south entrance was by a stile opposite College Lane. References to this stile occur in the records of the Court Leet. There are only two monuments worthy of note. One is an obelisk erected in 1838 to commemorate a tragic fire at the Castle Inn when six female servants lost their lives. The other, also an obelisk, is to the memory of Edward Farmer, the author of a once-popular and pathetic ballad entitled "Little Jim," the thatched cottage of the poem being at Polesworth. Edward Farmer, who was employed as a detective on the Midland Railway, was said to have "a versatility which was amazing, for he would dash off impromptu verses with the utmost facility upon almost any subject, grave or gay; his patriotic songs and pathetic ballads have been sung everywhere, and many a tear has been shed over the recitation of 'Little Jim'." He was very popular with his fellow townsmen. In his later years he resided at Derby, where he died in 1876.

Although not connected with the Parish Church—in fact, it is now associated with the Parish of Wigginton—it may not be out of place to refer here to the Spital Chapel in Ashby Road. It was founded and endowed by Philip Marmion in 1274, being dedicated to St. James and served by a master and four brethren of the Premonstratensian Order, who were to celebrate services for the repose of Marmion's soul. When the pestilence or Black Death visited the town in 1349, the chapel seems to have been converted into a hospital, becoming known as the Hospital of St. James, hence the present name of "The Spital." At its dissolution in 1547 the chantry chapel was valued at £3. 6s. 8d. In 1758 it was described as having been converted into a barn. In 1855, Edward Steere, afterwards Bishop of the Universities Mission, Central Africa, attracted by this ancient building, came to Tamworth and purchased it, with a few acres of land. His intention was to make it the abode of the newly-founded Guild of St. Alban. He found the chapel in use as a cottage, with two or more fireplaces and chimneys and an upper room in the roof, presumably a bedroom. All these signs of household occupation were removed, and a substantial brick wall with two windows facing west was erected. Foundations of buildings were traced on the south-west side. The building adjoining Ashby Road, now known as Spital House, was built for the purpose of a printing-house for the members of the guild, and it was intended to build three similar blocks, cruciform in design, but the proposal was abandoned owing to lack of funds. This building has been used as a dwellinghouse ever since. The Spital Chapel was restored in 1914 and is used for occasional services.

Chapter VI

THE CORPORATE ESTATE

THE TOWN HALL

THE TOWN HALL was erected by Thomas Guy in 1701. In the sixteenth century there were two town halls. It has been mentioned in a previous chapter that prior to the incorporation of the Borough under Queen Elizabeth's charter of 1560, when it came under one jurisdiction, the Warwickshire and Staffordshire parts of the town had their own officers and court leet, each part having its own town hall. The one for the Staffordshire side stood on the south side of Lichfield Street at the junction of the present New Street and Brewery Lane, and that for Warwickshire was on the north side of Market Street, where the Peel Arms Hotel now stands. Each thus stood within its own county. The one in Lichfield Street was discontinued in 1560, although it was used for other purposes until it was demolished in 1701.

A town hall must have stood on or near the site of that built by Guy, no doubt being built after the other halls were discontinued, for the minute of the Council accepting his offer, dated 19th September, 1700, reads as follows : "Whereas our worthy benefactor, Thomas Guy, Esq., hath declared that he will at his own charge erect a new Towne Hall in the Market place of this Towne in such manner as may be most convenient and most for the advantage of the towne and because such new Hall cannot be erected without pulling down the now present Hall and some other buildings belonging to this Corporation and also without taking down a house of Ezra Allens and a shopp of John Banes, therefore to encourage soe good a worke, we the Bayliffs and Capitall Burgesses doe order agree and declare that the said now present towne hall shall be taken downe and also soe much of the buildings belonging to the Corporation as are near the Towne Hall and found necessary to be removed in order to placing such new hall and that care be taken to agree with Ezra Allen and Mr. Banes to buy in their interest in order to place the new hall more commodiously and we do agree that Mr. Guy hath libertie to dispose of the materialls of the old hall at his own pleasure.''

Guy must have made use of the materials of the old hall as authorised by the Council, for when the floor in his own hall was being repaired in October, 1896, the removal of the floor boards for inspection revealed a portion of floor containing the inscription "1672. Robert Blake and Cornelius Osborne, Chamberlains" and the letters "C.R." As the board was found in the north-west corner of the hall, it must have been covered when a dais was constructed.

The Town Hall as built by Guy consisted of one room only, standing, as now, on large pillars. Access was obtained by an outside staircase at the eastern end. This staircase, in two sections, led to a platform which was used for official pronouncements and election addresses. The room proving to be insufficient, two more were added on the eastern side, the expense being met by public subscription. These two rooms were demolished in 1811, being inadequate, and two larger rooms were substituted, the first Sir Robert Peel giving £500 towards the cost and the Corporation paying the remaining £200. These rooms were further enlarged in 1845, and the present entrance on the south side was made. The clock in the front wall of the Town Hall was given by Mr. John Robins of Tamworth Castle in 1817. The space underneath the main room was used for the part of the market known as the Butter Market, butter and eggs being sold there. It was enclosed in 1835, and later, when the Tamworth Voluntary Fire Brigade was formed, the fire engine was housed there. The space was re-opened to the public in 1940 when a new Fire Station was built in Lichfield Street.

The principal room, which had been used for the meetings of the local governing body since its construction, was furnished as a Council Chamber in 1934, after a meeting at which the horse-shoe-shaped trestle tables then in use collapsed and sent some municipal visitors sprawling. It then ceased to be used for social functions and public meetings. A small gallery which was used in the days when hectic meetings were held at election times was closed a long time ago. The room contains several paintings and copies of the Borough Charters. A full-length painting of Sir Robert Peel, twice Prime Minister, hangs in a central position over the fireplace. Sir Robert made many of his political speeches to his constituency in this room, and it was from one of the western windows, over-looking the Market Place, where his statue now stands, that he declared his conversion to Free Trade principles.

A painting of Thomas Guy hangs on the opposite wall. It was given by Sir Charles Mansfield Clarke, Baronet, of Wigginton Lodge, in 1852. Another painting is that of Captain Sir William Peel, third son of Prime Minister Peel. He was a commander in the Naval Brigade in the Crimea and in India, and was severely wounded in the relief of Lucknow, dying soon afterwards. He was one of the first to receive the Victoria Cross, the award being made on 24th February, 1857.

Other paintings in the room are those of Mr. John Peel, Member of Parliament for Tamworth, who died in 1872 ; the Reverend Francis Blick, Vicar of Tamworth for 46 years until 1842 ; Mr. William Robinson, Mayor of Tamworth in 1841, 1852 and 1863, and the Reverend John Rawlet. The latter, who was a native of Tamworth, bequeathed the painting to the Borough by his will made in 1686, with other bequests, including his many books to form a public library for the benefit of the scholars in the town.

The room opposite the Council Chamber is known as the Mayor's Parlour, but as the Council's administrative offices are in Church Street it is little used for such purpose.

The cellars underneath the Town Hall, converted into public conveniences in 1908, formerly contained cells for prisoners, but the accommodation became unsuitable and thereafter prisoners were committed to the county gaol. The stocks and pillory stood in the Market Place in front of the Town Hall ; when their use was dis-continued they were stored in the cellars and later a caretaker broke them up for firewood.

The Town Hall, in addition to its use for civic purposes, has been used for the local courts and the County Court ever since its construction. The building was scheduled as an Ancient Monument in 1934, and because of its importance as such the Ministry of Works made a grant of £4,650 in 1957 to enable the Corporation to carry out extensive repairs to that part of the hall which had been built by Thomas Guy.

THE MUNICIPAL OFFICES AND THE ASSEMBLY ROOMS

The Town Hall becoming inadequate for public and social functions, it was decided that the best way to commemorate Queen Victoria's Jubilee in 1887 was by the provision of better accommodation. Emphasising the need for a new hall, the *Tamworth Herald* said : ''We wonder what a chance visitor must think of the motley assemblage of rickety rough benches, broken chairs and three-legged stools which do duty for seats at lectures, concerts, etc. The mere thought of them excites a shudder. An outside entrance is needed to the upper part of the hall, to what is a veritable death trap in case of fire.''

Suggestions were made for the removal of the Town Hall and the erection of a new hall in Market Street, but there was strong criticism. It took a long time to dispose of the question, and it was not until two years after the Jubilee that the commemoration was finally realised. The Corporation in 1888 purchased a large house, No. 21 Church Street, and four cottages adjoining, with adjacent grounds and a lodge and entrance in Aldergate. Part of the grounds was used for the new public building, the cost of which was met by public subscription. This building, which became known as the Assembly Rooms, was opened on 8th October, 1889, by Mr. Philip Muntz, first Member of Parliament for the Tamworth Division of Warwickshire.

The building contains a large room and gallery, a stage and dressing rooms, and a room which was formerly called a Supper Room but is now used as a Civic Restaurant. The Assembly Rooms now need to be extended, as they are inadequate for certain functions.

No. 21 Church Street came into use as Municipal Offices, and the cottages adjoining were demolished to make way for the construction of a new street which was named Corporation Street. The offices are now far too small for the town's administration, some departments having to be housed elsewhere in the town. A new building to include all departments under one roof in less crowded conditions, a Council Chamber and committee rooms, and better accommodation for the Courts, is badly needed. The existing Town Hall could then be used for other purposes, probably a local museum, which would be better housed there than at the Castle ; the latter could then be more fittingly kept to display furniture in keeping with the periods when the building was used as a private residence.

The Corporation purchased property known as Bradbury Square, adjacent to Aldergate Cemetery, in 1900. The houses were demolished and the site was used to extend Corporation Street so as to give through communication between Church Street and Aldergate.

THE PUBLIC LIBRARY

It might be said that the first public library in Tamworth was created in 1686 by the will of the Reverend John Rawlet, who made a bequest of his books to "the minister and schoole master of the towne of Tamworth" should they think them worthy of acceptance "to fix them in some roome belonging to the schoole of Tamworth or other convenient place there, that they may be preserved for the use of succeeding schoole masters and such students of the towne as shall need them and that it may serve as encouragement to others to make addition thereto, that there may be a public library for the benefitt of schollers in the said towne."

A catalogue of the books, 934 in number, is still in existence. The library was housed in a room in Guy's Almshouses, Lower Gungate, until 1868, when it was transferred to the then newly-constructed Queen Elizabeth's Grammar School in Upper Gungate. In 1932 the Trustees, with the consent of the Charity Commissioners, sold the library by auction and applied the proceeds to the purposes of Rawlet's Charity.

The Reverend John Rawlet was born at Tamworth in 1642. It is recorded that he was a man distinguished by his many and great virtues and his excellent preaching. He was for many years a lecturer at Newcastle-upon-Tyne, and died in 1686.

In 1804, a library known as the Permanent Library was established in premises in George Street. It was open to subscribers paying an entrance fee of two-and-a-half guineas and an annual fee of one guinea. Palmer, in his *History of Tamworth*, says that within a few years the library contained upwards of two thousand volumes. In 1893 it was merged with the Public Library then held in the Municipal Offices.

The next development in the library service came in 1841, when Sir Robert Peel, then Prime Minister, founded a library and reading room in premises in Colehill, opposite Church Street, on a site now occupied by the new Post Office. He performed the opening ceremony himself, stating that all persons over the age of fourteen, without distinction of political or religious opinions, were entitled to become members upon payment of one shilling quarterly. He said that it would be open to females, for it would be a gross injustice to the well-educated and virtuous women of the town and neighbourhood to presume that they were less capable than their husbands or brothers of profiting by the opportunities of acquiring knowledge. In 1866-7, according to the local press, there were 170 members and issues were 6,000 per annum, and it was announced that "all classes of men may enjoy a good fire for twelve hours a day and a first-rate supply of daily and weekly papers for the low charge of one shilling per quarter, paid in advance." In 1871 the library was transferred to rooms at No. 21 Church Street, but was closed in 1874 owing to lack of subscriptions and funds.

"Penny Readings" in connection with the Peel Library were commenced in the Town Hall in November, 1865, and had an audience of about one hundred persons at the first meeting. They were a great success, for at the third meeting "about six hundred persons contrived to squeeze themselves into a space scarcely large enough to hold three hundred comfortably, and many could not get admission." There were readings from Scott's *Marmion*, Charles Lamb and *Pickwick Papers*, with songs and piano solos. Said the local press : "Great praise is due to the numerous ladies and gentlemen who at personal inconvenience come forward to show the working-classes that it is possible to spend a pleasant evening in an agreeable manner without the assistance of the bottle and unaccompanied with the evils attending the gin palace.'' A month later it was recorded that more than a thousand persons presented themselves at the door of the Town Hall, so that hundreds were unable to gain admission. The readings continued for five years.

The first Act enabling local authorities to assist in the provision of public libraries up to the limit of a halfpenny rate became law in 1850. This limit was increased to a penny rate by another Act passed five years later, but it was not until 1881 that steps were taken by the Corporation to adopt the Act. A poll of the ratepayers was taken, a majority voted in favour of the adoption of the Act, and on 20th December, 1881, the Council voted a penny rate and appointed a committee to establish and manage a library. As a penny rate produced only £40 in those days, and the annual expenditure was estimated at £130, public subscriptions became necessary. The premises in Colehill formerly occupied by Sir Robert Peel's library were secured, and the library was opened on 3rd October, 1882. It was said at the opening ceremony that Tamworth was the smallest borough in the country to adopt the Act. There was a good response by the public, it being reported that within ten days 139 borrowers' tickets had been issued and 250 volumes borrowed, and that the reading rooms had been fully occupied, being full to overflowing in the evening. There were two reading rooms, one for smokers and one for non-smokers. The library remained open until 10 p.m. ; this was eventually altered to 9 p.m.

A society called ''The Tamworth Ladies' Book Society'' existed during the period when there was no library, but was discontinued in 1866 and its remaining funds were devoted to the purchase of books for the public library.

The Corporation having acquired No. 21 Church Street for use as Municipal Offices in 1888, the public library established at Colehill was transferred there in the following year. In 1905 the present building in Corporation Street was constructed, the cost, £2,000, being met by the gift of Mr. Andrew Carnegie. The new library was managed by a voluntary committee, but on 9th November, 1917, the Council took over the direct control and appointed a Library Committee.

The library service has expanded considerably during the past ten years, and the rooms have been re-arranged. They now contain adult and junior lending departments, a reference department which includes a local collection, and a newspaper room. Today the library has a membership of about four thousand.

CORPORATION ESTATES

The Bailiffs and Commonalty had power under their charter of incorporation to purchase lands and property. They must have begun to acquire corporate estates at an early date after receiving power to do so, for the civic records contain many leases of corporate property in the seventeenth century. In 1603 there were two leases of shops "on the north side of the new Town Hall under the same hall at the upper end next to the market cross"; 1613, lease of a tenement on the south side of Market Street "together with the stalls standinge and bulkes in the said street thereunto adjoining"; 1632, lease of land called Hillcroft, near Ladybridge Bank; 1634, lease of two shops near the Castle Gate (Market Street); 1636, lease of three shops in the Market Place on the north side of Market Street; 1649, lease of part of the King's Ditch "six score and ten yards in length and six yards in breadth in Perrycroft Lane (now the northern part of Marmion Street); 1662, lease of land in Catt Lane (a lane running parallel with Church Street from Aldergate to the Parish Church) and lease of a cottage and garden in Bowbridge (Bolebridge) Street; 1700, lease of land known as Bayleys Leas "lying in Fazeley alias Phazeley"; 1701, lease of part of the King's Ditch in Schoolhouse Lane (Spinning School Lane); and 1704, lease of three houses on the south side of Market Street to Thomas Guy. There are many others but these are given as an indication of the extent of the possessions of the Corporation.

A list of rentals compiled by the Chamberlains in 1774 shows that the Corporation then owned ten houses and shops in Market Street, five houses in Bolebridge Street, four in Church Lane, three in Aldergate Lane, two in Lichfield Street, and no less than nineteen in Stony Lane (Upper Gungate).

On 5th October, 1820, there being then no general power for local authorities to acquire land, the Bailiffs and Commonalty obtained a licence from the Crown to purchase houses and shops in Market Street from Mr. John Robins, then the owner of the Castle. The licence recites that the Bailiffs and Commonalty had been advised that although the charter granted by Charles II gave them power to acquire land to a certain value, they had been advised that they could not safely proceed to purchase these properties without obtaining a licence from the Crown. The purchase was completed on 24th April, 1821, and the properties have remained in the possession of the Corporation ever since. The Council sold other properties in Market Street to provide the funds for this purchase.

In 1891 the Corporation bought land in Salters Lane from the Trustees of Sir Robert Peel to establish a depot for their highways department ; they also built two cottages for the use of employees. Previous to this they had a depot at Glascote, but they sold the land to allow the present boys' school to be built.

The first housing scheme was carried out in 1900, the Council then exercising powers under the Housing and Working Classes Act, 1890, which had been passed following the report of a Royal Commission on the housing of the poor. The site selected was at the lower end of Lichfield Road, then just within the Borough boundary. The land in that area had been known as the Bradfords for several centuries. In fact, the lower part of Lichfield Street, before being re-named Lichfield Road, was known as Bradford Street. A new street, given the name of Bradford Street, was laid out and twelve houses were erected for the rehousing of families living in an insanitary area known as Bradbury Square, now occupied by part of Corporation Street.

No further building of houses took place until after the first World War, when house-building became a duty of all local authorities, an Act having been passed in 1919 to bring housing law up to date and to introduce government subsidies. The local housing shortage compelled the Borough Council to utilise the remainder of their land in Bradford Street, thirty houses being built in 1920-21.

The demand for houses continued, but sites within the Borough as it then existed were not easy to obtain, the only available land being in the Leys, but that was then considered to be serving a useful purpose as allotments. Also, the Ministry of Health at that time refused to sanction further building within the Borough on the ground of general unsuitability in comparison with available sites outside the town and the congestion within the Borough. At that time the density of population per acre was one of the highest in the country. Prior to the first World War there had been increasing development to the north of the town, in the Parish of Wigginton, gradually changing its rural character owing to its situation as the highest part of Tamworth and the shortage of sites within the Borough. The Council decided to purchase land lying between the Ashby and Wigginton Roads. In 1922, fifty houses were constructed there, and four years later the development of the site was completed by two further schemes containing ninety houses and a shop, and new roads named Borough Road and Willington Road provided a link between the Ashby and Wigginton Roads.

Upon the completion of this estate, the possibility of using any unbuilt land within the existing boundary was again explored, an attempt to secure an extension of the Borough having failed some years previously. The only available site within the Borough, an area of eleven acres including "The Leys Field", was acquired. The Leys is the name given to the district lying to the west of Aldergate, and in former times was known as the Castle Orchard. Two schemes of 146 houses were carried out in 1929-30 on this site.

Notwithstanding the number of houses so provided, the demand for new houses still continued ; in fact, right up to the commencement of the second World War. Again faced with a shortage of sites within the borough boundary, it was necessary for the Council to purchase further land outside, although a few months later the site came within the extended Borough, the Boundaries being altered on 1st April, 1932. The land selected was in Bolehall, then part of the parish of Bolehall and Glascote, and lay to the north of Amington Road. Upon this site of twenty-six acres, 326 houses were erected in 1932-33.

Another site of twenty-one acres in the same district, lying between Amington Road and Glascote Road was purchased and 160 houses were built in 1937-39. The outbreak of war stopped further building, but in 1948-49, 104 additional houses were built, completing the development of that estate.

The suspension of building during the war resulted in the

97

waiting list for houses being increased considerably, and a new site had to be obtained ready for the recommencement of building operations. In a desire to build up the large area of land lying between Tamworth and Fazeley, a site of twenty-six acres adjoining Fazeley Road and Bitterscote Lane was acquired, and in the years between 1947 and 1951, 250 houses and three shops were erected.

The state of the housing application list still necessitating the building of houses, yet another site had to be obtained. The Council decided to again build in the northern part of the town, and forty-two acres of land lying between Comberford Road, Gillway and Wigginton Road were purchased in 1951. This estate, the largest yet constructed, contains 525 houses and eight shops.

At the present time, land is being purchased for the development of a very large housing estate south-west of Comberford Road.

A scheme for the erection of dwellings for old people is now proceeding in Lichfield Street near the Moat House, and it is also proposed to construct flats on land in Bolebridge Street adjacent to the River Anker.

The Corporation now owns 1,800 houses and 26 shops.

Part of the old corporate estate, acquired so long ago that no records of the purchases exist, still remains—a field known as the Catcholme, two houses in Bolebridge Street, one in Church Lane, one in Orchard Street, one in Lichfield Road, and land near Bolebridge. Eighteen other houses, in Stranraer Place and Lochryan Place near the Hospital, were purchased in 1943.

In 1928 the Council purchased land in Lichfield Road from the Trustees of Sir Robert Peel ; the part near the Staffordshire Moor was converted into a recreation ground, and the remainder was continued in use as allotments.

Bolehall Park was a gift made in 1923 by the Reverend William MacGregor, a former Vicar of Tamworth, to the Parish of Bolehall and Glascote, and came into the possession of the Corporation when the boundaries were extended in 1932.

BURIAL GROUNDS

The Parish Churchyard was closed by Order in Council dated 15th December, 1876, but it was becoming full at the middle of the century, so in 1851 Miss Hester Wolferstan gave to the Vicar and

Churchwardens, the Mayor and the Town Clerk for the time being, a site for a cemetery in Aldergate upon trust to take the necessary measures for the consecration of the land according to the rights and ceremonies of the Church of England and at all times for ever thereafter to permit it to be used, occupied and devoted for the purposes of a burial ground exclusively for the inhabitants of the township of Tamworth and of the township or liberty of Tamworth Castle. She herself lived at the Castle at that time.

The Aldergate cemetery became full in the course of twenty-five years, being closed by Order in Council issued on 9th December, 1876. At a meeting of the Vestry of the Parish of Tamworth held on 11th November, 1873, it was decided to form a Burial Board for the Borough for the purpose of obtaining a new burial ground for the use of all the religious denominations. In 1875 the Board purchased land in Wigginton Road which is still used as a cemetery. It was also proposed to erect chapels as well as a Cemetery Lodge, but the Vestry refused to sanction another loan. The Borough Council decided to take over the powers and duties of the Burial Board in 1895, and the cemetery then came into the ownership of the Corporation. The cemetery has been extended on two occasions. In 1914 the Council proposed to erect a chapel in the cemetery owing to the distance from the churches in the town, but the outbreak of war caused the scheme to be abandoned.

In 1901 the Council agreed to accept responsibility for the maintenance of Aldergate Cemetery, the Trustees desiring that it should be maintained as an open space for the benefit of the inhabitants. For a time the cemetery was kept open for such use, but later, as control became difficult, it was kept closed. In 1952 the Council, making use of its powers in respect of disused burial grounds and after obtaining a faculty from the Bishop of the Diocese, laid out the cemetery as a "Garden of Rest." This development has been much appreciated by the public and has made a notable feature in the centre of the town.

The Council have also adopted a scheme for converting the Parish Churchyard into an open space as a "Garden of Rest," similar to Aldergate Cemetery, and it is proposed to carry out the work within the next two years. This will also create a desirable improvement in the centre of the town.

CHAPTER VII

HIGHWAYS AND TRANSPORT

IN EARLIER TIMES the inhabitants of a parish or manor were required to give their labour for the repair of the king's highways, except where a tenant was responsible as a condition of tenure of his land. In 1555 it became necessary to lay down measures for securing the repair of highways, and an Act was passed placing the responsibility upon the parish through which the highways passed ; the Vestry of the parish appointed from among the parishioners an unpaid surveyor who had the unpleasant task of requiring every inhabitant, who had to provide his own tools and materials, and horses and carts if he had any, to give four days' labour in a year— later it was increased to six days—it being the duty of the surveyor to inform the Justices of the defaulters. This system, called "statute labour," was much disliked and was therefore abused, as it became a common practice for persons to evade their duties by employing and paying someone else. There were also complaints that the surveyors pleased themselves which roads they repaired, often choosing by-lanes instead of main routes, that owners of land charged excessive prices to the inhabitants for the stones which were used for repairs, and that encroachments reduced the width of the passageways.

In the middle of the eighteenth century, there grew up a new system, that of the turnpike roads. As traffic between large towns increased, main roads became impassable owing to their neglected condition, and persons with an eye to business applied to Parliament for powers to enable them to repair roads and to impose tolls on those who used them, to provide the necessary revenue. Turnpike trusts were therefore created to control main roads, and gates and bars were erected to facilitate the collection of tolls. The period of operation of a trust was usually limited to twenty-one years but could be renewed.

Locally, a trust was created in 1770 to control what were termed "The Tamworth Roads." These roads were (1) Moxhull Park corner—Fazeley-Tamworth-Elford-Alrewas ; (2) Bassett's Pole—Tamworth ; (3) "Bird-in-the-Hand," Gungate, Tamworth— Two Gates—Over Whitacre ; and (4) Silver Street, Tamworth— Hopwas—Lichfield. Further Acts extending the period of the trust were passed in 1782 (extending the first period of 21 years by a similar period), in 1812 (for another 21 years), and in 1832 (for a further period of 31 years).

These local Acts gave the Trustees power to erect tollhouses, gates and turnpikes, and also side-gates across any lane or way leading into a turnpike road, and to collect tolls in respect of horses, cattle, coaches, wagons and carriages. Tolls were payable once only in respect of the same horses, etc., on any one day, reckoned from midnight to midnight. Double charges could be imposed on Sundays. Exemptions from tolls were granted in respect of funerals, attendance at church on Sundays, vehicles used in carrying certain materials for the use of the inhabitants, cattle going to and from pasture, post-horses carrying the mail, and horses of soldiers. In one of the Acts exemption was given from tolls along the road from Gungate to Two Gates in respect of carriages going to or from any of the coal-pits within the hamlet of Wilnecote or the Liberty of Tamworth Castle, or in the parishes of Grendon, Polesworth or Baddesley Ensor. There were penalties for evading tolls, or for permitting passage over private land to enable a person to miss the tollgate.

The Trustees had power to remove the High Bridge, Little Bridge and Foot Bridge near Lady Bridge, and to purchase land for widening the roads, and their Surveyor had authority to take materials for repairing the roads from rivers, brooks, waste land or from any private land not forming part of a garden, orchard, yard or park, compensation to be assessed by the Justices if not agreed.

The Acts authorised the Trustees to require the performance of Statute Work in repairing the roads by such inhabitants as were liable, with power to compound for the payment of sums to release them from the work. The Act of 1832 stated that no money was to be spent in repairs, improvements or cleansing streets in the Borough of Tamworth.

A map of the Tamworth Turnpike Roads, dated 1842, shows that tollgates were then in existence near Lady Bridge at the junction of Bonehill Road and Fazeley Road, Kettlebrook hill, and Amington Road near the railway viaduct. The Trustees had power to lease the tolls annually, which they did ; the sum paid for the Lady Bridge gate and Kettlebrook gate, let jointly, was about £400 per annum.

The Tamworth Turnpike Trust came to an end on 1st February, 1883. The balance of £387. 4s. 3d. in hand at that date was divided among the various authorities at a rate of seven guineas per mile, the proportion for the Borough of Tamworth (then a smaller area) being £16. 10s. 9d. The tollhouses at Lady Bridge and Kettlebrook Road were removed to widen and improve the highway, the former being sold to Sir Robert Peel. In the winding-up the Trustees resolved ''that the wheelbarrows and tools used by the men lately employed on the roads be given to them as a means of assisting them to gain a livelihood.''

Turnpike trusts were also formed in 1759-60, before the formation of the Tamworth Turnpike Trust, in respect of the road from Tamworth to Ashby-de-la-Zouch, and from Tamworth to Market Bosworth via Polesworth.

A description of the roads in the Tamworth area appears in *The Rural Economy of the Midland Counties*, written in 1796 by William Marshall. It says : ''The roads of this district had, it is probable, remained in a state of almost total neglect, from the days of the Mercians, until some twenty years back ; when a spirit of improvement went forth. Its principal road, from Tamworth to Ashby, lay in a state almost impassable, several months in the year. Statfold Lane''—this was then the name given to Ashby Road from the Fountain in Upper Gungate—''had long been proverbial. In winter it was unfrequented ; the riding and driftways, at least, being on trespass, thro the adjoining inclosures. Waggons were dragged on their bellies through it : to a coach it was impassable, during the winter months ; and might still have laid in that state, had not a material, which is seldom used in this intention, been applied to its amendment : namely, SAND : . . . the base of the road being levelled, the sand was laid on, eighteen inches to two feet or more thick, according to the nature of the bottom, on which it was laid.''

A reference to the mail coach route is contained in the minutes of the Corporation for 29th November, 1826 : ''The Bailiffs having received letters and Mr. Telford's report and a plan of the intended mail road from London to Liverpool from Mr. Secretary Peel''— the second baronet was then Home Secretary—''ordered that the thanks of this Hall be transmitted to Mr. Peel for his kind attention to the weal and interest of this Borough. Ordered that the Members for this Borough be requested to wait upon the Postmaster-General to state the anxious desire of the inhabitants of Tamworth that the road should go through the town according to Mr. Telford's original plan as a contrary direction will materially prejudice its local interests.''

At that time the mail route from London to the north-west came through Atherstone on the Watling Street, then diverting to Tamworth before proceeding to Lichfield. At Wolseley Bridge beyond Rugeley, the Holyhead route proceeded via Stafford and to Liverpool via Stone, Knutsford and Warrington. There was also a route to Holyhead from London via Stonebridge, Coleshill, Bassett's Pole and Lichfield to Wolseley Bridge. The Corporation minute would seem to refer to a proposal to construct a new road from Meriden to Canwell to alter the Liverpool route, but the scheme was never carried out.

The construction of the railways had a material effect upon the operations of the turnpike trusts, as the new method of travel reduced the amounts collected from tolls and the public began to resent the restriction upon their freedom in the use of the highways. Waking up a sleepy tollgate keeper would be an annoyance, and the payment of dues would be irksome. In the meantime an Act which became the basic highway law for over a century, the Highways Act, 1835, enacted that the repair of roads constructed before that year should become the responsibility of the parish but through the rates instead of by the direct labour of the inhabitants, and a new system of highway authorities, amended as time went by, came into existence.

When turnpike trusts were abolished, the law required that the cost of repairing such roads should be borne by the county as well as by the parish. They became known as main roads, being roads which gave communications between large towns, and the contribution required to be paid by the counties was based on the principle that through traffic had a material benefit. The whole cost of repairing and improving such roads, now known as county roads, is borne by the county council.

To-day the duties of a highway authority are many and varied. They include road maintenance and scavenging, drainage, street lighting, the making up and adoption of private streets, the repair of footpaths, the prevention of encroachments and obstructions, the naming of streets and the numbering of houses, the removal or repair of ruinous and dangerous buildings, the protection of public rights of way, the provision of parking places for vehicles, and the observance of building byelaws designed to give safety and to protect public health.

Turning to local conditions, we find that "paving grants" giving permission to "the Bailiffs and proved men of Thomeworth" to take tolls of certain goods coming to the town for sale, in aid of paving the town, were granted by Edward II, Edward III and Henry VI.

Highway nuisances and encroachments were dealt with by the Court Leet in former days. The Court rolls contain many entries such as the following :—"Geoffrey Clede is in mercy because he made a pigsty and a hedge to the harm of the king's highway," "Walter of Gumpegate (Lower Gungate) is in mercy because he unjustly made a wall in Saltereslone (Salter's Lane) to the harm of the king's highway" (11th June, 1294) ; "It is ordered that the dung heap opposite the Church be removed or whoever likes may freely carry and take it away" (11th November, 1297) ; "It is ordered under pain of 2s. and the forfeiture of anything found that women who sell the entrails of oxen or other animals shall not henceforth throw out dung or other rubbish at their doors to the harm and abomination of passers-by" (20th November, 1304) ; "No one from henceforth may hold a stall in the highway at the cemetery gate, or put their manure below the cemetery (the Parish Churchyard) under pain of half-a-mark" (30th October, 1318) ; "Alan Drambel has made a well in the highway to the harm of the

town, therefore in mercy 4d,'' ''Robert Juet has made an encroachment with manure and timber in the king's way by the church wall,
therefore in mercy and to remove the nuisance within eight days''
(10th May, 1319) ; ''It is ordered that no one on the Warwickshire
side or on the Staffordshire side shall put manure on the highway at
the Carrefour'' (18th October, 1331 ; the Carrefour was the junction
of Church Street, Aldergate, Silver Street and Lichfield Street, and
the county boundary ran through it) ; ''Ordered that no bakehouse
(or oven) be put up in the highway beyond one week under pain of
half-a-mark'' (20th April, 1347) ; ''Robert Ropere fined 2d. for
stopping up the common gutter by the Swynemarket'' (13th October,
1388) ; ''Ordered that each tenant by the Swynemarket shall clean
the gutter around the pavement and see that the pavement there
does not worsen under pain of 40d. each'' (26th October, 1389) ;
''John Lovell is presented for putting waxwater in the common
gutter to the harm of all the neighbours'' (14th November, 1380).
An order made in 1546 prohibited wagons or carts being left in the
highway on feast days.

It would seem that householders were required to assist in
keeping the streets tidy, for on 25th October, 1511, it was ordered
that ''each inhabitant well and sufficiently clean before his entrances
every three weeks ; penalty 4d.'' The period of three weeks coin-
cided with the meetings of the Court Leet. On 21st October, 1550,
a further order was made, this being written in English : ''Let
every man make cleane the strettes before their dorrz'' under penalty
of 4d. for each offence.

It is possible to obtain the old names of many of the streets
from the Court Leet rolls, and references made to them hereafter
are extracted from that source. For centuries, as now, the centre
of the town has been the rectangle which includes Market Street,
George Street, Colehill, Church Street and Silver Street. Market
Street formerly had no houses on the south side, being open to the
Castle and separated from it by the Castle ditch. In 1285 Philip
Marmion made an encroachment to the detriment of the King's
market with his Castle lands, so it would seem that there were no
houses on the south side at that time. George Street was known
as Bullstock or Bullstake Street, there being a bull-ring at the
junction with Bolebridge Street and Colehill ; a record in the rolls

dated 6th May, 1314, refers to a house opposite the bullstake. The south side of George Street consisted mainly of gardens. Common Lane, called Agate Lane, was a public way to the river. The lane was widened in 1898. College Lane, between George Street and Church Street, was in 1420 called Cocket's Lane. Colehill was called Cross Street, receiving its name from the Stone Cross which stood at the junction with Church Street and Lower Gungate; an order made by the Court Leet on 12th October, 1516, forbade butchers to sharpen their knives on the cross. A grant of a burgage in 1370 by Sir Baldwin de Freville described it as being at "le stonene cros," and extending from the highway to the land of the Dean of the Collegiate Church of Tamworth. The present Church Street was formerly two streets, the part between Colehill and the Parish Church being called Butcher Street, as it contained the Swine Market near the junction with Lower Gungate, while the other part, from the church to the Carrefour, was known in 1295 as High Street. It was called "Churchestrete" in 1377. There is a reference in the rolls for 12th June, 1424, to a house in Church Street extending to "Catteslone" (Cat's Lane) which ran from Aldergate opposite the Methodist Church, to the Parish Church, parallel with Church Street, and in 1314 to the surrender of a messuage lying by the Carrefour and "Elregate" and extending to the lane leading to the church. This lane continued as a footpath along the present Halford Street to Moor Street and thence to Coton across the Staffordshire Moor, then continuing as a lane, which was diverted when the railway was constructed. Silver Street was called Ladybridge Street.

The passage between Church Street and Market Street near the Town Hall now known as Middle Entry was made a public right of way in 1805 as the result of an approach by the Corporation to the owner of the property, Lord Townshend. It would appear from the correspondence, however, that the passage had been used by the public previously.

Lower Gungate was called "Gumpiyat" and "Gumpegate." Little Church Lane was known as "Chirchelone," and the lane now called Church Lane was formerly known as Schoolmaster's Lane, probably because the Grammar School adjoined it. The lane on the opposite side, now called Spinning School Lane, appears as

Colehill

From engraving by E. B. Hamel, 1829.

Schoolhouse Lane in a perambulation of boundaries made in 1697 ; ten years previously, as the minute book of the Common Hall records, Lord Weymouth gave a barn and land for the construction of a building for the purpose of putting children to work. Palmer, writing in 1845, describes this lane as leading to Amington Hall. There is still a public footpath to Amington Hall *via* the Station Fields, and it therefore seems that the lane was connected to this footpath before the Railway Station was built, and that the path would then be diverted to facilitate the construction of the two railways.

The land to the east of Lower Gungate consisted of gardens. Beyond, at the boundary of the borough, where Marmion Street now runs, lay the King's Ditch. The Victoria and Albert Roads were not constructed until after the coming of the railway. These roads derived their names from the visit of Queen Victoria and her consort Prince Albert to Drayton Manor, where they were entertained by Sir Robert Peel in November, 1843.

The continuation of Lower Gungate, now called Upper Gungate, was known as Stony Lane. Aldergate in 1294 was called "Elregate," and in 1424 "Ellergate." As late as 1813 it was called Eldergate Lane. The area on the north side now known as The Leys, which began to be extensively developed in 1888, was formerly the Castle Orchard.

Lichfield Street appears under that name in 1384, but the lower part was called "Otewell-strete" or Outwall Street in 1290. The part of Lichfield Road near the River Tame was known as "Bradeford" (1290) arising from the Broad Ford at that point. The area is still known as the Bradfords, but Bradford Street is now the side street containing a Corporation housing estate. Brewery Lane, with the part of New Street leading to the River Tame, was known as Wyburne Lane in 1318.

Palmer suggests that the ditch constructed by Offa was the site of the earlier fortification of the town, that there was a defensive wall on the town side of such a ditch, and that there were posterns or bars in the Holloway, Lichfield Street near New Street and Brewery Lane, Gungate at the junction with Aldergate, and possibly in Bolebridge Street, but nothing can be found in any records to prove that Offa re-fortified an existing ditch.

The first reference to Lady Bridge, which crosses the River Tame below the Castle, occurs in the rolls of the Court Leet for 11th June, 1294 : "It is ordered that the makers of trypes (tripe or entrails for sale) henceforth do not wash their trypes except by the lord's bridge, where it will not be harmful to the town, upon pain of 12d." There was, and still is, a public right of access from the Holloway to the river at the side of the bridge. It was then called "the Bridge of our Lady," and later was known as "St. Mary's Bridge." The Court Leet annually appointed an officer or warden to take charge of the bridge ; thus we find that on 2nd December, 1318, "Robert, son of Robert Slorecockes, who had custody of Lady Bridge by Tamworth, came and surrendered his custody into the hands of the bailiffs and community of Tamworth, together with all right that he had in the said custody of the said bridge." The appointment of a warden for the bridge continued until the incorporation of the borough.

Included in the civic records is a bond entered into with the Bailiffs and Capital Burgesses on 23rd May, 1694, by Richard Weaman, whereby he undertook to repair such part of the bridge as lay within the borough, during the term of fifty years if he should so long live, upon payment of the sum of forty shillings per annum.

The bridge, which was a long, narrow structure of twelve arches, with barely sufficient width for a single vehicle to pass over, was destroyed by floods in 1795 ; a new bridge was completed four years later.

Lady Bridge formed part of the boundary of the borough until 1932 ; one half belonged to the Corporation and the other half to the County of Stafford. Until it became a county bridge in 1929 its reconstruction or repair caused difficulties, particularly in the days before county councils came into existence and an order had to be obtained through the County Quarter Sessions. In order to ensure the repair of bridges, and to settle responsibility, an Act passed in 1531 placed the liability for repair on the counties or the corporate towns in which a bridge lay ; the liability was divided where a bridge lay in a county and a corporate town, the county justices being empowered to enquire who was responsible for repair and to make presentments in cases of default. Sir Robert Peel made a handsome contribution of £500 towards the Borough's share of the cost of widening Lady Bridge in 1840.

Bolebridge, which spans the River Anker, also appears in very old records. The bridge which was replaced in 1877 was believed to have been in existence in the time of the Marmions ; it was a very narrow stone bridge, provided with recesses where foot passengers took refuge when vehicles passed. The present bridge was constructed by the Staffordshire County Council in 1935.

The minutes of the Bailiffs and Capital Burgesses contain the following entry dated 18th March, 1826 : ''An indictment against this Corporation having been preferred at the last Warwick Assizes for not having kept Bowbridge in good repair and condition but suffering it to become ruinous in decay and dangerous for His Majesty's subjects to travel upon, it is ordered that the indictment be defended upon the part of the Corporation under the advice and opinion of Counsel and that the Town Clerk take such measures to defend the Corporation against the said indictment as Counsel should advise. Ordered also that the parapet walls of the bridge where they are now too low be raised by solid masonry to a safe and proper elevation on both sides of the bridge and that the foundations, the arches and the piers of the bridge be carefully examined by a competent architect and that such repairs as shall be found necessary be well and effectually perfected as soon as the season of the year will permit.''

The inhabitants of the Warwickshire part of the Borough were the subject of a decision at Warwick Quarter Sessions in 1653. They had been required to pay their contribution to the cost of repairing certain bridges in the County of Warwick but, with two other Warwickshire boroughs, had not paid their quota, ''by reason that those corporations, lying upon the chiefest rivers of this county, are enforced to repair several great bridges belonging to their own corporations, therefore declared that for the reasons aforesaid ought now to be spared and order that the sums payable by those Corporations shall be payable by the whole county, the same corporations excepted.'' The Warwickshire burgesses of Tamworth were therefore successful in pleading that they had enough to pay for in repairing Bolebridge.

Two years later, William Allen, surveyor of highways for the

Warwickshire part of Tamworth, reported to Warwick Quarter Sessions that he had disbursed several sums of money for the repair of the highways and that the inhabitants refused to make a levy for his reimbursement ; it was ordered "that Waldive Willington, Esquire, one of the justices of the peace for this county, shall be and is hereby desired to examine the accounts of the said William Allen and ascertain what is due to him, which being done the said inhabitants are hereby required forthwith to make a levy for the reimbursement of the said William and the several persons therein taxed are forthwith to pay their several proportions to the said William Allen and herein they are not to fail." Waldive Willington was Governor of Tamworth Castle when it was held by Cromwell's forces in 1643.

It would appear that the streets were repaired by contract at some time, for in 1696 John Brittain, who was given an annual payment, had neglected his work, and in 1754 it was agreed to pay Thomas Brittain and Thomas Glover seven pounds per annum for twenty-one years to keep the streets and causeways in good repair.

Reference has been made to the right of public access to the river at the side of Lady Bridge, and in Common Lane. Similar accesses were available in Wyburne Lane (now Brewery Lane and New Street) and in Bolebridge Street. There was a lane in Bolebridge Street called Catcholme Lane, being opposite the field known as the Catcholme on the other side of the River Anker. A minute of 1762 refers to it then as a watercourse, "formerly a lane and called Catcholme Lane," and a further minute of 1769 shows that it was near the Red Lion Inn. The river access in Common Lane was called Agatewater-leader. The washing of "trypes," permitted at Lady Bridge, was prohibited at Agatewater-leader, the wife of Richard le Fleshewere being fined in 1297 for allowing her servants to wash the entrails of oxen there. The prohibition was repeated by an order made in 1332. There used to be a footpath from the end of Wyburne Lane to Lady Bridge, but in 1829 the Bailiffs and Capital Burgesses granted an application by Mr. Robins of the Castle to "build a strong wall from the river end of the common lane in Lichfield Street along the river edge up to Lady Bridge so as to enclose the narrow strip of land between the river and Mr. Robins' bowling-green garden," now the Castle Bowling Green.

During the eighteenth century there was a proposal to extend the navigation of the River Trent. On the 7th October, 1760, a petition to the Honourable George Townshend was signed by the Bailiffs, the Town Clerk and 83 inhabitants, they "being of opinion that the extending of the navigation from Burton-upon-Trent to Tamworth must be of publick utility, serviceable to the Town, and advantageous to your property, beg leave to recommend the consideration thereof to your regard." On 17th February, 1766, a further document signed by some of the inhabitants was sent to Lord Townshend and Lord Weymouth with reference to a Bill for making the Trent navigable through Staffordshire, stating that it must be of great advantage to the country in general and to Tamworth in particular, and asking for their lordship's directions as to how they should proceed in the matter. On 4th March, 1785, the Bailiffs and Capital Burgesses gave their consent for "a navigation to be made by the rivers and over the land belonging to the Corporation," and ordered "that the House of Commons be immediately petitioned for leave to bring in a Bill for the making the rivers of Trent, Tame and Anchor navigable, and the Bailiffs and Town Clerk are hereby authorised to affix the common seal of this Corporation to such petition." No further record appears in the minutes.

Canals were brought into the district towards the latter part of the eighteenth century. An Act was passed in 1768 to construct a canal from Coventry to Fradley Heath, to link up with the Trent and Mersey Canal, but it was not until 1785 that the canal was extended from Atherstone. This became known as the Coventry Canal. In the same year Birmingham was linked to this canal at Fazeley, that portion being given the name of the Birmingham and Fazeley canal. These canals form the present boundary of the borough on the east, south and west.

The pavements of the town were flagged for the first time in 1808, and byelaws were then made with a view "to preventing damage and to secure to foot passengers the sole use and enjoyment of the pavements." One interesting point about these byelaws, as compared with those in force to-day, is that one-quarter of any sum recovered by penalty was to be given to the person who should first give information to the Bailiffs or the Town Clerk, and the remainder was to be used in keeping the pavements in repair.

In the days of the stage-coach, Tamworth had communications with the big towns. A handbook issued in 1818 shows that at that time coaches started from the King's Arms (now the Peel Arms Hotel) to London every day at 2 a.m., to Liverpool daily at 7 a.m., to Manchester daily at 9 a.m., to Birmingham on Sundays, Tuesdays and Thursdays at 1.30 p.m., and to Nottingham on Mondays, Wednesdays and Fridays at 10.45 a.m.

The Midland Railway, then known as the Birmingham and Derby Junction Railway, was opened on 4th August, 1839. It had necessitated a long viaduct over the Anker near Bolebridge. Then came the London and North-Western Railway, linking Rugby and Stafford and giving access to London and the north-west without having to travel *via* Birmingham. It is unfortunate that the situation of the crossing of the two lines, being affected by the River Tame and the differing levels, prevented a junction being constructed, as it would have given a much better railway service with consequential improvement in the development of the town. An embankment for the purpose of linking the two lines on the east of the town was later constructed, but no rails were ever laid as the project was abandoned. The "Trent Valley Line" was opened in 1847 and the first turf was cut by Sir Robert Peel, when Prime Minister, in a field of his own adjoining the Staffordshire Moor at a ceremony held on 13th November, 1845. George Stephenson was present at this ceremony.

As in the case of other market towns, transport of passengers from the neighbouring villages in the nineteenth and the first part of the twentieth centuries was by horse-drawn brakes. The first motor omnibuses in Tamworth appeared in 1914. Their advent necessitated fixed stopping places, and for many years the vehicles used the Market Place for omnibuses proceeding from Fazeley and Lichfield, while those coming in from Kingsbury used the open space in Bolebridge Street known as the Knob. As the services grew, the accommodation became far too small and there was serious traffic congestion. In 1930 these arrangements were discontinued, and Corporation Street became the omnibus terminus. This also, in course of time, became totally inadequate, and in 1955 an omnibus station was constructed on land lying between Corporation Street and Aldergate, thus creating an excellent improvement which was welcomed by the travelling public. Today, frequent services link the town with the surrounding villages and with Birmingham, Sutton Coldfield, Nottingham, Lichfield, Nuneaton and Coventry, and there is a daily service to Hull, London and Liverpool.

Chapter VIII

THE DEVELOPMENT OF PUBLIC HEALTH

ONE OF THE OUTSTANDING FEATURES of the past century in local government has been the improvement in the conditions affecting public health. In earlier times manorial courts dealt with such matters as the sampling of food and the making of byelaws or orders to prevent nuisances. The decisions of the court leet in Tamworth referred to in another chapter give instances of this. It was not until towards the middle of the nineteenth century that public opinion demanded an improvement in public health conditions. In most towns there was no drainage system, no means of fighting infectious disease, water supplies were inadequate and polluted, and the absence of building control encouraged the erection of back-to-back houses, dingy courts and cellar dwellings.

The prevalence of cholera led to an investigation into the health of the towns. It revealed an unsatisfactory state of affairs and resulted in the passing of the first Public Health Act (1848) and the establishment of a national General Board of Health, with power to set up local boards. This first attempt to assert national control did not meet with much success, as many towns objected to what they thought was interference in local matters. In Tamworth, a meeting of the Town Council had been held on 23rd September, 1846, to consider what measures ("if any," says the minute) could be taken to effect the underground drainage of the public streets, and a letter to the Mayor from Sir Charles Clarke, who lived at Wigginton Lodge, was read, stating that he had learned that bowel disorders, important in their character, and fatal in their results, had prevailed in Tamworth and that the health of the inhabitants must have been materially affected by the want of underground drainage, and the consequent exposure of a large quantity of putrid matter upon the surface of the streets, the effect of the decomposition of animal and vegetable substances ; he offered a subscription of one hundred pounds in the event of measures being taken to free the town from the existing nuisances, and mentioned that a similar subscription was offered by Miss Wolferstan, who tenanted the Castle. The Council resolved that their thanks be given for the liberality and kindliness in making the offers, but did nothing else ; Sir Charles Clarke sent his subscription, and six years later, "owing to there being no work on drainage at the time," the Mayor was instructed to confer with him as to the use of the money. The minutes do not say what the Council did with it.

In 1854 the General Board of Health, after a visit by one of their inspectors, proposed to make an order requiring the establishment of a local board of health under the Act of 1848. This drew forth a strong protest from the Council, and they submitted a petition to Parliament against the Act being applied to the town ; as is often the case, rates came into the matter, the petition alleging that "local charges would necessarily be increased to an extent which must be positively ruinous and unbearable." In a letter to Lord Townshend, one of the local members of Parliament, asking for his support, the Town Clerk expressed the hope that Lord Townshend and Sir Robert Peel (the other member) would together "blow the enemy out of the water." The petition must have been successful, for there is no record of any order having been made.

The General Board of Health was abolished in 1858, and in that year another Act was passed authorising the establishment of local boards of health by the voluntary decisions of the inhabitants.

On 10th November, 1862, the Council, evidently anxious to control nuisances, resolved to appoint the Inspector of Police for the Borough as Inspector of Nuisances at a salary of £2 per annum. This appointment must have been declined, unless the official resigned later without any record in the minutes, for on 24th September, 1863, a police-sergeant was appointed to the office at an increased salary of £4 per annum.

On 24th September, 1863, a meeting of the Council was held to consider "whether any and what steps can be taken for improving the drainage and health of the town,'' and it was resolved that every attention was being paid to the subject, ''very many nuisances having been abated and the general health of the town being much improved.'' However, six months later, as a result of a requisition from the required number of ratepayers, it was decided to set up a local board of health. The board, soon after its establishment, decided that it was necessary for carrying out the provisions of the Act that the drainage of the town should be connected with a water supply.

Alas, it took sixteen years to provide a water supply, and over forty years to create a proper drainage system ! At a public local inquiry held by the Local Government Board in 1872, it was revealed that twenty years previously, when the town suffered from a severe visitation of smallpox, a Government inspector had reported that out of 5,036 yards of streets, only 2,405 were drained and that very imperfectly ; that he had condemned the sanitary condition of the town as exceedingly defective, had pointed out that the health of the town would be much improved by proper supplies of water and drainage, and had recommended that the Act of 1848 should be applied. It was further revealed at the inquiry that an application made in 1866 for sanction to a loan of £1,500 for repairing the streets was refused until the sanitary state of the town could be attended to. Another glimpse of the conditions at that time is given in a speech by the Mayor on 5th August, 1871, in which he said that as cholera was fast approaching, it behoved them to be prepared for it by improving the sanitary condition of the town, which, from his personal inspection of the ''back slums,'' he found to be shocking, many people in Bolebridge Street being confined to their beds from the effects of the effluvia from foul drains, cesspools, ashpits and pigsties, and he gave a warning that if cholera broke out in their present condition it would be fearful for the town.

A full-time Surveyor and Inspector of Nuisances had been appointed for the first time in 1864 ; ten years later the person then holding the office reported that ever since his appointment he had watched the drainage of the town and with the increasing population the drainage got worse ; he was convinced from his experience that unless a thorough system of drainage was adopted, and a good supply of water obtained for flushing the sewers, they would one day have an epidemic which would not be easily removed.

Such lack of progress was not confined to Tamworth ; it is mentioned as an indication of the position which prompted the passing of an Act (1875) which became the basic law of public health for sixty years, following the report of a Royal Sanitary Commission in respect of which a member of the Town Council truly observed that the recommendations of the Commission would be one of the most effective and sweeping measures talked of for years.

In 1879 it was stated that most of the wells in the Borough were polluted owing to the nearness of drains, privies and cesspools, and an analysis showed impregnation with sewage matter. A surgeon said that during the thirty-three years he had been in practice he could distinctly trace illnesses arising from the impurity of the water, and could give instances without number where whole families had been attacked with typhoid fever from impure water ; there were scarcely a dozen wells in Tamworth from which pure water could be obtained and it was impossible, on account of the formation of the land, for the wells to be otherwise than impure unless there was a proper system of drainage.

It was not until November, 1878, that the Borough took a decisive step to obtain a water supply. The Rural Sanitary Authority, in a search for water resources for their own residents, had made a boring at Moor Farm, Amington, three years previously, but the water then found was so saline as to render it useless. A further boring at Bolehall east of the railway viaduct produced an inadequate supply. Another trial boring at Coton in 1878 produced no water, but later in that year a boring in the sandstone strata at Hopwas was successful. Steps were then taken to purchase land for the purpose of sinking a well, and at that stage the Borough Council, having received a deputation from the Rural Sanitary Authority, decided to join the scheme. A Joint Committee of the two authorities was formed and given delegated powers to establish and manage a water undertaking.

The sinking of the well, which was commenced on 5th May, 1879, proceeded to a depth of 165 feet ; on 12th September a shot was fired into the sandstone rock and water then rose to a height of 38 feet in as many minutes. The well had a capacity of 750,000 gallons, with a yield upon test of about one million gallons a day, and the water was pumped across to Glascote, where a reservoir had been constructed. Mains were laid throughout the town and district, and the supply to consumers began in July, 1881.

The increasing consumption of water caused the Joint Committee to give consideration in 1917 to the question of increasing the supply. Four years later, it was decided to sink a new borehole adjacent to the well, and additional pumping plant was installed, the work being completed in 1926. A second reservoir was constructed near the Pumping Station in 1936.

In 1940 it again became necessary to increase the supply. After expert consideration of all possible water resources in the district, that at Hopwas now being known to be limited, it was revealed that there was no site within the Joint Committee's area which could be recommended with any confidence as being likely to yield an additional source of water of such quantity and quality as would justify the erection of a second pumping station. The Committee therefore had no alternative but to make arrangements with the South Staffordshire Waterworks Company, whose mains were within a reasonable distance, for a continuous supply in bulk to Hopwas to supplement that of the well so as to meet the ever-growing demands of the town and district.

Although the problem of providing a pure water supply was met in 1880, the need for a system of sewage disposal continued and was the subject of heated discussion for at least another twenty years. Such sewers as then existed or were gradually being provided drained into the rivers or elsewhere. In 1864 plans for a drainage system were prepared, but nothing was done. Further plans were prepared in 1868, and again in 1875, but still without any result. In the latter year the Council began discussions with the Rural Sanitary Authority with a view to establishing a joint system for the town and district. Four years afterwards the Council passed a resolution that it was desirable to construct a complete system of drainage, but thirty years were still to elapse before such a system was in operation.

In the meantime, unsatisfactory conditions prevailed. A Medical Officer of Health was first appointed in 1872. In his annual report for 1882 the then Medical Officer said that in some of the streets the open channel gutters were often filled with soapsuds and other waste water, that sometimes the washings of a yard or slaughterhouse ran across or alongside the pavement, and that the smells were at times very sickening. The Local Government Board, noting the report, warned the Council that delay in making any necessary provision for the health of the Borough in the matter of drainage would fix a very heavy responsibility upon them. The *Tamworth Herald* referred to epidemics of scarlet fever and smallpox which had occurred in the town twenty years previously, when it was considered that the cause was defective sanitary arrangements, and yet, it said, they were still faced with their old friend, "the sewerage question."

The discussions with the Rural Sanitary Authority lasted nine years ; a joint scheme was prepared, but although it reached the stage of a local inquiry for the purposes of loan sanction, the scheme was abandoned in 1884 on account of the expense, and the Committee which had prepared it for the consideration of the two authorities was dissolved. It must be admitted that the Borough took the initiative in this breaking-up of the proceedings, on the grounds that "the rates are already high ; drainage is unnecessary, the town being already one of the healthiest towns for its size in the United Kingdom." The Local Government Board, to whom complaints were made as to the lack of a sewerage system, held an inquiry but decided that the evidence given did not appear to justify them in holding that the Council were in default within the meaning of the Public Health Act, but that the Council had admitted that they were without a proper system of drainage, and recommended that the question of a joint scheme should again receive consideration.

Notwithstanding the advice of the Local Government Board, many years passed before the subject was again re-opened. At last, agreement was reached in 1905 between the Corporation and Tamworth Rural District Council whereby, although each authority would be responsible for the sewers necessary to drain its own area, a joint sewer was to be constructed for the purpose of carrying the sewerage from those sewers to a pumping station to be erected at the Bradfords in Lichfield Road, from which it would be pumped to Outfall Works to be constructed at Coton for treatment and disposal. The scheme was carried out in 1908. A little ceremony was held by the Corporation in the Holloway in January of that year to mark the commencement of the digging in connection with the new

Borough sewers, and it was then stated that as the first meeting to consider a sewerage scheme was held on 17th April, 1874, no one could complain that they had been rushing the work !

In 1892 the Borough combined with Tamworth Rural District in building an Isolation Hospital, for the treatment of infectious diseases, on land adjoining the Warwickshire Moor at Bolehall. This Hospital passed into the ownership of the State under the National Health Service Act, 1946.

Reference has been made to the importance of the Public Health Act, 1875. This and later Acts gave local authorities powers and duties in respect of the abatement of nuisances, the inspection of food, bakehouses, slaughterhouses, dairies, etc., the removal of house refuse, the supervision of common lodging houses, the regulation of offensive trades, the provision of public baths, the supervision of housing conditions and many other matters affecting public health. Much could be said about the carrying out of such functions, but they are common to all authorities, and it would be impossible to place on record all the details affecting the local administration of these services. It is appropriate, however, to refer to slum clearance, as it has played an important part in improving the public health of the town.

An Act passed in 1890 made provision for the making of orders for the closing or demolition of insanitary houses, and for the making of schemes for the improvement of overcrowded and unhealthy areas. Under this Act the Corporation condemned and demolished certain dwellinghouses, including an area known as Bradbury Square, part of the site of the present Corporation Street.

It was not until 1930, however, that "slum clearance" measures were adopted on a larger scale. Under the Housing Act of that year, local authorities were required to make inspections of their areas with a view to the removal of insanitary houses. It can be said that the Council were keen to improve the town by taking advantage of the new measure, for even before the Act became law they had prepared a programme designed to be operated over a period of several years. During the nine years which followed before the outbreak of war in 1939, many courts and alleys were condemned and removed or closed. These included Marshall's Court, Church Street, adjacent to the Baths and Institute, Hall's

Row, Aldergate, near the Congregational Church, Matthews'
Yard, Aldergate, opposite the Methodist Church, Middle Entry
(between Church Street and Market Street) and several areas in
Bolebridge Street, including Paradise Row (between Mill Lane and
Bolebridge Street) and the Tan Yard.

Since the war, more properties have been dealt with, including
Queen Street, Arched Row and Tenters Croft, all lying between
Bolebridge Street and the River Anker, and also houses in Church
Street near the Parish Church. Another programme for the
clearance of unfit houses has been prepared, involving nearly five
hundred houses. The carrying out of this programme, like the
previous one, will cause considerable changes in the appearance of
the town.

Public baths, regarded as an important part of the public health
service, were not provided in the Borough until the last decade of
the nineteenth century. The first arrangement for the provision of
Baths was a private one, an enterprising townsman, Mr. Williams,
setting up in 1884 an establishment at the corner of College Lane
and Church Street, offering "steam, rain and shallow baths and
ordinary tub or shower baths, during the hours of 6 to 10 daily,
with a reduced charge for working men."

In 1885 the Rev. William MacGregor, then Vicar of Tamworth,
erected the Baths and Institute in Church Street at his own cost.
The building contained a swimming bath and private baths. These
were managed on a voluntary basis for a few years, and in 1891
the Corporation took over the management by renting the Baths.
In 1909 the building containing the baths was given by the owner to
the Tamworth Industrial Co-operative Society, but in the Deed of
Gift he gave the Corporation the right to use the Baths during the
summer months until they ceased to use and occupy them or until
they had public swimming baths of their own.

These Baths served a useful purpose, but the swimming bath
had to be operated on "the fill-and-empty without treatment
system," that is to say, the water in the bath was changed twice
weekly, with the result that there were only a few hours per week
when bathers had the opportunity of bathing in clean water, for
which a higher charge was made ; those patronising the baths at
other times had to be content with dirty water, the only compensa-

tion being a lower admission fee. As the baths were filled from the public water supply, they had to be closed in times of drought to conserve the supply.

In 1935 the Council had to give consideration to the question of providing new Public Baths, as those in Church Street were proving to be hopelessly inadequate, and there was a grave risk of infection through bathing in contaminated water. Owing to the increased popularity of open-air bathing, it was decided to construct an open-air swimming pool in the Castle Pleasure Grounds which, since their development five years previously, were rapidly becoming the centre for sport and recreation. Arrangements were made for the water to be chlorinated, and heated in cold weather. These baths quickly became popular, and today are used by bathers from a very wide area.

CHAPTER IX

THE WATCH; THE FAIRS; THE GRAMMAR SCHOOL; THE FIRE BRIGADE; GAS AND ELECTRICITY; EDUCATION; THE POOR LAW; THE CIVIC MACES

THE WATCH

IN THE CHAPTER dealing with the proceedings of the Court Leet a reference is made to the obligations of the burgesses to serve as watchmen on command of the Bailiffs. They were assisted in their duties by a constable appointed annually by the Court Leet. After the incorporation of the borough the control of the watchmen and the constable came under the Bailiffs and Capital Burgesses.

The minutes of the corporate body give further instances of the regulation of the watch. It appears that by the eighteenth century the practice of requiring the burgesses to undertake such duties had ceased and that supervision of the town during the night was restricted to the constable, who was also called the Bellman, for on 5th July, 1790, it being found that this was insufficient for protection from thieves and other disorderly persons, it was ordered that all inhabitant householders must take their turns in keeping watch, either in person or by employing substitutes. The duration of the watch was fixed at from 11 p.m. to 4 a.m. from April to September, being extended to 5 a.m. from October to March, and they were required to patrol and perambulate the whole inhabited part of the Borough twice in each night. One watchman in addition to the constable was required during the summer and two during the winter. The constable was authorised to select householders before the hour of two o'clock in the afternoon of the day when duty was to be performed, and he was required to give warning either by word of mouth or by notice in writing delivered at the house of the person selected. Substitutes under 18 or over 50 years of age, or who were "weak in body, infirm, lame or otherwise unfit" were not allowed. Men over 60 not rated to the Poor Rate were exempt, as also were women if they were not so rated. The penalty for refusing to watch was five pounds.

Upon the new corporate body taking office in January, 1836, the watch, as well as the Council, was brought up to date by a decision to provide the watchmen and constables with a lantern, a staff and a rattle, one of the constables with three pairs of handcuffs, a pair of leg chains and a staff, and the other constable with a halbert, staff, and a pair of handcuffs.

Procedure was tightened up on 1st August, 1840, when it was resolved by the Council that the watchmen should be supplied with a book with instructions to enter therein every night the names of persons whom they suspected of being out for any illegal purpose whatever, whether for theft, mischief or poaching, and to make sure that there was adequate supervision the watchmen were ordered to produce this book for the inspection of the Mayor at his house between nine and ten o'clock every Monday morning, and, in his absence, to the next senior magistrate who might be at home.

Shortly afterwards it was decided to discharge the constables and watchmen, and two police officers were appointed at a salary of one pound per week, less the cost of uniform calculated at three shillings per week. A Superintendent of Police was also appointed at a salary of £20 per annum. By resolution of the Council, the constables were equipped with a cutlass and a belt, a staff, two pairs of handcuffs and a cap, all to be produced for the inspection of the Watch Committee when it was thought proper. They were required to serve full-time and not to engage in any other business ; they were both to be on duty until midnight, and one of them, in his turn, until 3 a.m.

The generosity of the Council was extended to the provision

of goloshes in 1851, with an instruction that the police were to use them during the night. It was also ordered that all pick-lock keys in the possession of the police be given up, and that all keys taken from suspicious persons in future, if not required in evidence, must also be given up and handed to the Mayor.

In 1840 a law was passed authorising county justices of the peace to organise police forces for the whole of the county, but in 1856 this was made compulsory. In consequence a constabulary for the County of Stafford was formed, and an agreement was made between the Council and the county justices whereby the police establishment of the Borough should be consolidated with that of the county as from 1st September, 1857 ; it was arranged that the police force for the borough should consist of two constables under the supervision of a superior officer, that the Chief Constables should make the appointments but that the constables, in addition to their ordinary duties, should also obey such orders as may be given by the Borough Watch Committee, and that the Borough should pay a contribution of £120 per annum. This could be regarded as the first transfer of functions from the Borough to the County.

THE FAIRS

In 1337 Edward III made a grant of two fairs, to be held on St. George's Day and St. Edward's Day, and the four succeeding days. This grant is the earliest of the various letters patent and charters preserved in the archives of the Corporation. It was confirmed in the charter of incorporation received from Elizabeth I in 1560, and in her second charter of 1588 a third fair, which became known as "St. Editha's Fair" or the "Cherry Fair" and is referred to in the chapter dealing with the Parish Church, was also granted. Of these three fairs, the Cherry Fair only is now held, and the date is 26th July, this being the original date as changed by the alteration of the calendar in 1752. St. Edward's Fair, formerly held on 13th October and changed to 24th October by the alteration of the calendar, was still being held on the latter date when Palmer wrote his *History of Tamworth* in 1845. William Marshall, author of *The Rural Economy of the Midland Counties*, records that he visited Tamworth Fair on 24th October, 1784, and that it was held principally for sheep. He noted that there were about five thousand sheep, with about a hundred head of cattle. "In the morning the sheep 'hung,' owing to a rumour of a great 'drop' in the London markets, a circumstance which shows how much, and how far, the markets of the kingdom are influenced by the metropolis. Notwithstanding, however, this unfavourable circumstance, and notwithstanding the fullness of the fair, the demand was such that every sheep (generally speaking) was sold by one o'clock, and at high prices, a proof that at the distance of one hundred miles the influence of Smithfield is weak, compared with that of the markets of the neighbourhood.''

On 13th August, 1852, the Council resolved that "a Statutes for the hiring of servants be established within this Borough, and that the same be held on the first Monday in October in this and every succeeding year.'' At the inauguration of this fair in the following October the remains of the old stone cross in Colehill were removed to make way for the roasting of an ox. The Council, having received a memorial from the burgesses, resolved on 1st February, 1854, that a "cheese and bacon'' fair be established; six months later they ordered that the fair directed to be held on the last Monday in October be held on 24th October, the old fair day previously mentioned, and that the same be duly advertised as a cheese and bacon fair "pursuant to the resolution of the last meeting,'' but an error appears to have been made in the writing of that record as there was no reference to any fair in the minutes of the previous meeting nor, in fact, since the resolution passed six months previously.

It would seem that by 1854 the fair granted for St. Edward's Day, like that of St. George's Day, had fallen into disuse, and that the fair which is still held on the first Monday in October is not really a charter fair at all, as has been supposed over a long period, but is the fair established by the Council's resolution of 1852.

In common with other towns, the fairs used to be held in the streets, causing much inconvenience as traffic increased, and in 1878 it was resolved that "the Tamworth Statutes be limited to one day and that the shows, etc., be allowed to come into the Market Place and streets after nine o'clock only on the Saturday night.'' The fairs were well attended. Describing the Cherry Fair in 1882, the

126

Tamworth Herald said : "The cattle began to arrive early in the morning, and not without considerable difficulty they were drawn up in lots in Church Street and Silver Street. Lichfield Street throughout its entire length was devoted to the horses, which were not arranged in lots as were the cattle, but on the other side of the street, thus affording the intending purchaser, and the public generally, a better opportunity of criticising them and judging their respective merits and demerits. The town during the whole day was thronged with people, but towards evening the principal thoroughfares became impassable. The whole town presented a thoroughly holiday appearance, and everyone seemed bent on enjoying themselves on the July fair day."

Fairs were regarded as events of great importance in the days when they were accompanied by public holidays. Markets and fairs were the principal means of people coming together for trade and enjoyment, and also for the public hiring of servants, which has long since been discontinued. In 1875 the *Herald* expressed satisfaction that the practice of servants having to appear at the fairs in order to obtain employment under contract for a year was on the decline, and said it was one of the old customs of which they should be rather ashamed than otherwise, as it meant servants exhibiting themselves in a public market and selling themselves to the highest bidder. Fairs have now become pleasure fairs only, and have lost much of their significance by the growth of modern attractions. In Tamworth, even the pleasure fairs are considerably smaller than they used to be. At the present time, fairs are also held in the Castle Pleasure Grounds at holiday times, but these are not related to the charter or to the grant which was made so long ago as 1337.

THE GRAMMAR SCHOOL

Reference should be made to the link which formerly existed between the Corporation and the Grammar School. The second charter granted to the town by Elizabeth I in 1588 ordained that there should be a grammar school in Tamworth to be called "the Free Grammar School of Elizabeth Queen of England in Tamworth" for the education, teaching and instruction of boys and youths in grammar in all future times to endure and with the intent that the school might be the better governed and continued the Bailiffs were incorporated as the Guardians and Governors, and the power of appointing "a fit and learned pedagogue" was granted to the Bailiffs and Capital Burgesses meeting in Common Hall. The Bailiffs therefore became the governors but the corporate body appointed the master. An ancient annuity or grant of £10. 3s. 2½d. per annum from the Crown towards the salary of the master was confirmed by the charter.

The school, however, was in existence before the days of Queen Elizabeth, although the exact date of its foundation is not known. Leland, the historian, in recording his visit to Tamworth in 1541 referred to in the second chapter, wrote : "There is a Guild of St. George in Tamworth, and to it belongs £5 land per annum, and of late one, Johne Bailie gave other £5 land unto it ; and therewith is now erected a school-house."

In his book, "English Schools at the Reformation, 1546-48," published in 1897, Mr. A. F. Leach names Tamworth Grammar School along with ten others as the oldest schools in the country. He states that they were founded before 1066, "though the dates assigned to them in the Report of the Schools Inquiry Commissioners vary from 1509 to 1652."

The school was situate in Lower Gungate opposite Spinning School Lane ; the houses now standing upon the site bear the town crest, the fleur-de-lis. The school was transferred to the present site in Upper Gungate in 1867.

The minutes of the Common Hall record some of the appointments of the schoolmasters by the Bailiffs and Capital Burgesses, including that of George Antrobus, who was master for forty-nine years and of whom an entry made in the Parish Register upon his death in 1708 said that his memory ought to be perpetuated to eternity. If such respect was shared by the Capital Burgesses, it did not prevent them from passing a resolution in 1680 reciting at great length that Mr. Antrobus had of late received several gifts and benefits of a considerable value from several benefactors and that in consequence the sum of forty shillings, which the minute made quite clear had been given to him as a gratuity, his predecessors never having been given such sum, would not be paid to him for the future, but would be used by the town chamberlains "towards

Free Grammar School

From engraving by E. B. Hamel, 1829.

part of a stocke for the setting of the poore of this town to worke'' ; and so the master of the Grammar School contributed involuntarily to public funds.

The minute book also records that in 1674 ''it was then ordered and agreed by the mutual assent and consent of the Bailiffs and Commonaltie without opposition that at the request and desire of Mr. George Antrobus now schoolmaster of the freeschoole of Tamworth and for other weighty reasons them thereunto moving, there shall be another bay of buildings added and erected to the schoolehouse for the inlarging thereof, the same being now too straite, and there shall be allowed him towards the charge of the same buildings and finishinge thereof the sume of eight pounds to be paid.''

The Capital Burgesses found it necessary in 1826 to require the Bailiffs to inform the schoolmaster, the Reverend Samuel Downes, that they disapproved of his conduct and to ''apprize him of their duty as guardians and governors of the school to protect the rights and convenience of the inhabitants as to the education of their children'' ; it would appear that he was neglecting the school and that it had declined in consequence. He was therefore requested to resign within a week, failing which the Bailiffs were instructed to give him six months' notice. Mr. Downes duly resigned. His successor, the Reverend Thomas Pearson Lammin, had to be informed that he must relinquish his curacy, ''it being impossible that he can perform the several duties of schoolmaster and curate of Tamworth simultaneously, but it is not intended to prevent him from undertaking any curacy which may require Sunday duty only.'' The Capital Burgesses also decided : ''With respect to the rules of the school it is ordered that the hours of tuition during the summer season shall be the same as those already ordained, but that the summer season shall be reckoned from 1st March to 10th October, and the winter season from 10th October to 1st March, during which last season the hours of tuition shall be from 9 to 12 in the forenoon and from 2 to 4 in the afternoon. With respect to holidays, the Saint days are abolished and also Easter holidays, and the holidays at Midsummer and Christmas shall be of six weeks' duration at each of those periods. There shall be two half-holidays in every week, one on the Saturday and the other at the option of the master.''

The Commission appointed to investigate the municipal corporations in 1833, at the time of municipal reform, made the following remarks in the report on Tamworth Corporation :—

"The bailiffs and capital burgesses have the right of appointing a master to the Free Grammar School of Queen Elizabeth in Tamworth. This school was in existence in the 2nd year of Edward VI and was then endowed with an annual stipend to the master payable out of the Crown Revenues for the County of Stafford . . .

"The condition of the School appears to have fluctuated considerably at different periods. In the report of the Charity Commissioners it is stated that the school having been previously very flourishing, gradually declined till, about ten years prior to their inquiry, it was altogether suspended during six months.

"A new master having been appointed, new rules were made by the governors with consent of the high steward, by which it was ordained that the master should teach all free scholars, or cause them to be taught arithmetic and writing, and also reading English and the principles of English grammar, and that he should be entitled to receive the sum of £4. 4s. 0d. per annum for each scholar so instructed. He also gave a bond conditioned to resign within six months after request, in writing, from the governor. Under this system the school revived a little for a time, but sank again to a very low ebb. At the time of the inquiry by the Charity Commissioners, September, 1823, there were only four scholars who attended for two hours in the morning, to be instructed in Latin, and then went to other schools to learn reading, writing and arithmetic, the master not undertaking this branch of instruction himself.

"The condition of the school has again become more flourishing. At the time of my inquiry, there were 24 free boys, besides four boarders. Regard being had to the limited extent of the endowment, this number of scholars appears highly satisfactory."

The Bailiffs ceased to be the governors of the school in 1836, upon the reconstitution of the Corporation, and Trustee-Governors were then appointed. The newly-constituted Council endeavoured to secure control by putting themselves forward in the appointment of the Trustees, but they were unsuccessful.

THE FIRE BRIGADE

There is no clear record as to when a fire brigade was first formed in Tamworth, although it has been said that one was established following a big fire at the Castle Inn in 1838, when six female servants were burned to death. The Council minutes show, however, that a voluntary fire brigade was taken over by the Corporation when a Fire Brigade Committee was first appointed in 1871.

At that time the fire engine was housed in a building in Hospital Street. In 1880 the Council gave permission for the space underneath the main room of the Town Hall to be used as an engine house. A fire escape was given by the Humane Society.

Until the nineteen-twenties, a horse-drawn fire engine was used ; the horse, being used by the Corporation in the collection of house refuse and in street scavenging, had to be fetched from duty upon the receipt of a fire call, so that the Brigade could not depart to the scene of the fire until the horse arrived. The out-moded conditions of the Fire Brigade service and the need for giving assistance to the rural areas led, in 1926, to a re-organisation in co-operation with Tamworth Rural District Council. A joint committee of the two authorities was formed, as had been done in the case of the local water supply and the disposal of sewage. A motor fire engine and up-to-date appliances were purchased, and premises in Lichfield Street adjoining the offices of the Rural District Council were used as a fire station. In 1940 a new fire station was constructed at the corner of Lichfield Street and Wardle Street.

Fire brigades were taken over by the Government during the second World War to form a National Fire Service. The local service never came back into the possession of the Borough and the Rural Authorities, for after the war the Government decided that fire services should be operated by county councils and county boroughs only, and so the Tamworth Fire Station had to be transferred to the Staffordshire County Council.

GAS AND ELECTRICITY

A company called the Tamworth Gaslight and Coal Company was formed in 1835 to provide a gas supply for the town and district. Gas-works were erected on land at the rear of Bolebridge Street.

Four years later the Corporation adopted the Lighting and Watching Act, 1833, the first Act to authorise street lighting, and gas street lamps were then erected. There was much talk in the nineteenth century that the Corporation should buy out the Company and establish a municipal gas undertaking, but no active step was taken to accomplish this.

The first Act permitting local authorities to apply for Provisional Orders to authorise them to supply electricity for public or private purposes was passed in 1882. Tamworth Corporation secured an Order in 1904, but the efforts then made to obtain a supply of electricity were unsuccessful. Not until 1924 did Borough residents have the opportunity of using electricity, and then it was through the enterprise of the Pooley Hall Colliery Company who commenced to generate electricity at their colliery at Polesworth, and laid mains in the adjoining district. The Council, exercising their powers under the 1904 Order, entered into an agreement whereby the company undertook to act as managers of a municipal electricity undertaking, and to lay cables throughout the Borough. The only criticism which can be made of the project is the choice of the site for a transformer station, the selection of land at the rear of the Public Library in Corporation Street being likely to interfere at some future time in the development of the adjoining land, and particularly in the extension of the Library.

The Corporation undertaking was necessarily small, being confined to the area of the old borough because the Company, and not the Corporation, exercised the powers of distribution in the rural district and in the part added to the borough in 1932. In 1934 the Council decided to sell the Corporation undertaking to the Company. By so doing, they were able, with the purchase price, to dispense with street lighting by gas and to substitute electric lamps. It was anticipated at that time that the day was not far distant when small electricity undertakings would be merged in larger ones ; after the war a policy of nationalisation, not amalgamation, was adopted by the Government. Local authorities which had to part with their undertakings to the State received no compensation except the transfer of outstanding loan debt, while Tamworth, in selling its undertaking in 1934, received a benefit which could not have been obtained otherwise.

EDUCATION

For half a century the Borough Council exercised certain limited powers with regard to education. School boards were established under the Education Act, 1870, for elementary education, but these were separate bodies, not being under the control of the local authority. In course of time it was found that education beyond the standard provided by the boards was needed, and so a Technical Instruction Act was passed in 1889 authorising local authorities to provide instruction in the principles of science and art applicable to industries and in the application of special branches of science and art to specific industries and employments. In 1893 the Tamworth Town Council appointed a committee, called the "Tamworth Science and Art Classes Committee," to provide education under the Act of 1889. They authorised the use of the small upper room at the Town Hall for a laboratory for science classes, although there is no record that classes were actually held there but it is known that soon afterwards there were science and art classes at the Baths and Institute in Church Street.

The Education Act, 1902, abolished the school boards and made local authorities responsible for both elementary and secondary education. Non-county boroughs with a population of over ten thousand were given powers over elementary education only, but as the population of Tamworth was below that figure the Staffordshire County Council became the education authority for the Borough. The Act nevertheless gave power to the Borough Council to spend a sum not exceeding a penny rate in supplying or aiding education other than elementary. At first the Council decided not to appoint an Education Committee as they had authority to do, but instead they resolved to act in co-operation with the County Council and "that the borough be made a local centre for secondary and technical education in the borough and the rural district surrounding it." They also decided to levy a penny rate for the purpose of providing scholarships at the Grammar School for Tamworth boys, the balance of the money to be used for the science and art classes which had been set up ten years previously. The County Council authorised the Borough Council to continue the administration of these classes at the Baths and Institute and also evening continuation classes which appear to have been then running at the Board Schools. In 1905 the Borough Council appointed an Education Committee to supervise the art and evening classes and to provide scholarships tenable at the secondary schools, the Girls' High School, when built, being included in this arrangement as well as the Grammar School. This Committee continued to function until the Borough lost these educational powers by the Education Act, 1944, which restricted local education authorities to the county councils and county boroughs.

THE POOR LAW

Although the municipal authority has never been responsible for the administration of the poor law, the Bailiffs and Capital Burgesses made certain decisions in respect of the relief of the poor.

The Relief of the Poor Act, 1601, formed the basis of the poor law system for over two centuries. It required the churchwardens and "four, three or two substantial householders, to be appointed by the justices, to serve as overseers," who were to meet at least once in every month in the church of the parish, "there to consider of some good course to be taken and of the sum meet to be set down" ; they were made responsible for setting to work the children of those who could not maintain them, and to set to work also such persons "as use no ordinary and daily trade of life to get their living by," and were given power to collect money weekly or otherwise by taxation of every inhabitant or occupier to purchase a convenient stock of flax, hemp, wool, thread, iron and other necessary ware and stuff to set the poor to work. They were authorised to bind children as apprentices until the age of twenty-four in the case of males, and until the age of twenty-one or until marriage in the case of females, and to build houses on the waste or common within the parish for the poor to live in. There was imprisonment for those who would not work.

In course of time the meetings of the overseers were held in the vestry, and this gave its name to the parochial authority which, meeting under the chairmanship of the incumbent, continued to exercise certain functions in a parish until the twentieth century. The Vestry now exercises no control in local government.

It has been mentioned that the selection of householders to serve as overseers of the poor was made by the justices of the peace under the Act of 1601. A peculiar situation arose in 1724. The Act entitled mayors, bailiffs or other head officers of corporate towns to have the same powers as the justices, so on Easter Monday the Bailiffs appointed two persons to be overseers for that year. About an hour after the appointment had been made, certain new justices appointed two other persons, and at Tamworth Quarter Sessions held about a month later the appointments made by the Bailiffs were quashed and those made by the justices were confirmed. Both parties of overseers acted under their appointments and assessed ratepayers to a rate, with the result that one ratepayer who paid his rates to the overseers appointed by the Bailiffs received demands from the other overseers and, naturally, refused to pay. In consequence the overseers appointed by the justices distrained upon the goods of the ratepayer, who commenced an action against them for breaking in and taking away his goods, namely, three pewter dishes to the value of 40s., and claiming £10 damages. At the hearing at Stafford Assizes before the Lord Chief Justice on 26th July, 1725, it was agreed that the parties should attend the Lord Chief Justice and be determined by him upon the single point of priority of appointment. This was done, but there is no record of any decision, although it would appear from the documents that the Lord Chief Justice was in favour of the Bailiffs.

As mentioned previously in this chapter, the Bailiffs and Capital Burgesses in 1680 discontinued paying the sum of forty shillings per annum to the schoolmaster of the Grammar School, Mr. George Antrobus, on the ground that it was a gratuity which his predecessors had never enjoyed, and they generously donated it instead to the overseers to find employment for the poor ; the involuntary contribution of Mr. Antrobus was then supplemented by a sum of three pounds "out of the Common Towne Stocke towards the encouraging and promotinge of such a good and charitable worke," but the town contribution, unlike that of Mr. Antrobus, was subject to be recalled or repaid as the Bailiffs or the majority of the capital burgesses thought fit.

The minute book of the Common Hall states that in 1687 Lord Weymouth gave to the town a barn and land in Schoolhouse

Lane for conversion into a house for setting poor children to work, and that as the cost would be considerable, it was ordered that a contribution of £20 be made out of the Chamberlains' box, and also four pounds per annum towards the cost of maintenance. The minutes for 1693 also record the continuance of a grant of £5 to the "Spinning School" (hence Spinning School Lane) from the town box, and the acceptance of the sum of £10 from Thomas Guy, for the same purpose.

On 26th June, 1712, the Bailiffs and Capital Burgesses ordered "that the Overseers of the Poor of Tamworth provide brasse letters of T.P. for such poor of Tamworth as receive weekly pay from the towne, first cutting the letters T.P. on cloth or flannel to be laid under the brasse letters and both firmly fastened on their right sleeve of their uppermost garment neare the shoulder, the charge to be allowed on the Overseers' Accounts." Lest it should be thought that this act on the part of the corporate body to stigmatise the recipients of poor relief was an idea of its own, it should be added that these letters, which stood for "Tamworth Pauper," were required to be affixed by an Act passed in 1697.

The Spinning School eventually fell into disuse and the Bailiffs and Capital Burgesses converted the building into dwellings for the poor. On 1st August, 1740, they made an order "that the Chamberlains shall use such measures as they shall be advised are proper to be taken to turn out all the Paupers who live in Corporation Houses." Although there is no record of the corporate property held at this time, it seems likely that this resolution applied to the converted building.

The need for a workhouse arose at about that time, for at a meeting of the corporate body on 10th May, 1739, it was decided that "whereas the poor of this Borough are become very numerous and exceeding burthensome to the inhabitants of the said Borough, it is therefore thought necessary and agreed upon at this hall that a workhouse be erected and built within the Borough for the better support of the poor and ease of the inhabitants thereof, and that the same be done by way of subscription and that a proper subscription paper be prepared for such Noblemen, Gentlemen and others who shall think fit to contribute thereto."

The workhouse was built by the Earl of Northampton in 1741

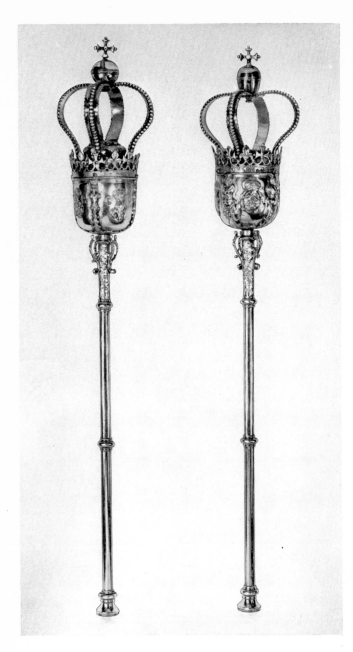

The Borough Maces, 1663

on land in Colehill opposite Church Street. The building was not used for more than a few years, becoming inadequate. It was then included in a charity given to the town by the Earl of Northampton, and was sold by the Trustees in 1914. A new Post Office has now been erected on the site.

A new workhouse at the rear of Lady Bank, later to become part of a brewery and now used as offices, was given to the town in 1750 by Lord Weymouth and Lord Middleton.

At about the same time that there was an outcry for parliamentary and municipal reform, there arose also dissatisfaction with the administration of the poor law. A Poor Law Inquiry Commission was formed in 1832, and two years later, when the Commission issued its report, an Act was passed establishing Poor Law Commissioners with power to group parishes, which had been the unit for poor relief since 1601, into unions under the control of elected Boards of Guardians. The Tamworth Union, which was then formed, consisted of the Borough of Tamworth and certain parishes in the rural district.

Boards of Guardians were abolished in 1929, when their duties were transferred to county councils and county borough councils, the term ''poor relief'' then becoming known as ''public assistance.'' These authorities, also, lost such powers in 1948 ; the poor law was abolished and ''national assistance,'' controlled by the State, took its place.

THE CIVIC MACES

Under the charter of 1663 two Serjeants of the Mace were appointed for making proclamations and arrests ''in like manner and form as the Serjeants of the Mace in our City of London do and execute them,'' each being given authority to carry a silver mace engraven and adorned with the royal arms.

Originally a mace was a weapon of warfare, but eventually it became a symbol of power and authority in ecclesiastical and governing circles, to indicate the person in whom the control of the body or organisation was vested. Corporate towns adopted the practice of giving their civic heads such a symbol, no doubt also because the mace was used by the Sovereign and the mayor could be regarded as his representative, being the chief magistrate and leader of the local community. To signify this connection with the royal power, the civic maces carried the royal arms and had other adornments.

Queen Elizabeth's charter authorised the use of two silver maces, but there is no record as to whether they were ever provided. If they were, they must have ceased to exist, for the maces now in use date from the time of Charles II, presumably being made following the granting of the new charter of incorporation.

The maces bear a head or bowl at the top of the shaft, crested with a circlet of fleur-de-lis, and surmounted by a crown ; the bowl contains, in addition to the royal arms (which are quartered, first and fourth, France and England ; second, Scotland, and third, Ireland) a rose, a thistle and a harp, and on one bowl the royal initials "C R" appear. On the base of each shaft is a fleur-de-lis, the crest of the borough, and the words "I V fecit," the initials of the maker.

CHAPTER X

MUNICIPAL ADMINISTRATION

T̲O THOSE WHO ARE INTERESTED in local government today, it is
equally interesting to note how the Bailiffs and Capital Burgesses
comported themselves as the governing body of their day. Before
the incorporation of the Borough in 1560, there was no municipal
council of any kind ; government of the town was vested in the
Bailiffs and their officers, these being appointed by the Court Leet,
which also made the byelaws, regulations and orders referred to in
the chapter describing the actions of that court. Some boroughs
had the title of Mayor from an early date, but in Tamworth the
Norman title "Bailiff" was continued right up to 1835, when
boroughs were "reformed" and were then officially given a mayor,
aldermen and councillors. For a brief period in 1688, when the
charter granted by Charles II had to be surrendered to his successor, James II, the title of Mayor was used under a new, short-
lived charter. There were two bailiffs for each part of the town—
Staffordshire and Warwickshire—but history does not record
whether the system of having two persons to exercise authority
caused any difficulties if they disagreed.

The Borough was incorporated under the name of "The
Bailiffs and Commonalty of Tamworth," and was given two
bailiffs and twenty-four "capital burgesses" (the equivalent of the
modern aldermen and councillors). They met in "Common
Hall." The capital burgesses were appointed for life, so long, to
quote the charter, "as they shall well behave themselves."

Unfortunately, the early records of the newly-constituted
corporation are no longer in existence, so reference cannot be made

to the activities of the capital burgesses before the period beginning with the charter of Charles II in 1663, from which year the minutes are available as a continuous record. In 1738, when the Attorney-General was called upon to advise the Secretary of State whether the right to nominate the Town Clerk vested in the Crown under the charter (which it did not), he reported : "Upon my inquiring what had been the usage in respect to the nomination of the Town Clerk precedent to the Charter of King Charles II, and subsequent to the attainder of the Earl of Essex," who had procured the second charter of 1588 from Queen Elizabeth, "it was alleged that the books of the Corporation being destroyed or lost during the Rebellion, they could not trace the usage further back than that charter." It would seem from this that the minute book for the period from 1560 to 1663 will never be found.

However, there is sufficient material in the minutes from 1663 to 1835 to know how the bailiffs and the capital burgesses regulated their meetings. In 1665 they decided that any member not present at the time appointed would be fined one shilling unless he could prove that he was prevented by some extraordinary occasion. No shirking of duties ! Three years later the fine was increased to five shillings. A century later the fine was again increased, this time to ten shillings, with an addition by the inclusion of any member "who shall depart before the Hall breaks up without leave of the Bailiffs." There was no question of a member attending for some spicy item in which he was interested, whether from curiosity or personal interest, and then leaving the others to cope with the rest of the business ! Another order made in 1698 required attendance throughout a meeting and the signing of orders to show how members had voted : "Every of the Capital Burgesses upon every lawful summons shall appear at every Hall that shall hereafter be called, and shall continue at such Hall until all the business intended at that Hall shall be agreed on and to sign such orders as shall be made or to pay for every neglect . . . unless he can give reasonable excuse to the Bailiffs and major part of the Capital Burgesses." The previous year an order had required that every dissenting member must sign as a dissenter and that every order not so subscribed would be void.

One wonders what Josiah Newey did by way of misbehaviour to cause him to offer the following apology to his colleagues on 12th

January, 1681 :—"Whereas I have in diverse wayes and upon sundry occasions, misbehaved myself whilst I had the honor of being one of the Capital Burgesses of this Borough of Tamworth, for which I acknowledge myselfe to have bin justly expelled from being a member of the said body and for which said offences and irregularities I doe hereby declare myselfe to bee heartily sorry ; seriously resolving never to commit the like for ye future ; and doe therefore request ye Bailiffs and the rest of ye Capital Burgesses to remit and passe by my aforesaid faults ; and that by their favour and goodnesse I may bee restored to ye place and office of a Capital Burgesse for which condescention I shall bee very thankfull." He must have been very sorry for himself.

Neglect of duty in attendance at meetings of the Common Hall is referred to in minutes passed in 1700. On 21st June, after a wait of an hour, the Serjeant-at-Mace was sent to fetch six absent members ; he found them all together "at an alehouse in the towne being Joseph Wilcox's house," but they did not comply with the request, for they sent an answer that "they desired to be excused at this tyme, which was in contempt of the authority of the Corporation and contrary to their duty." At a meeting called for the 29th July, only twelve out of the twenty-four members were present, so the meeting could not be held, it not being "a complete Hall, which is looked upon as a contempt and contrary to their duty." Perhaps the length of notice was at fault, for the minute records that the Serjeant-at-Mace gave them notice only the night before, for two o'clock next day. Another minute, dated 28th June, 1715, reveals that a member had been given notice to attend some ceremony, but "he not only refused to appear but very contemptuously told the Serjeant-at-Mace to tell his masters that he would not come, therefore for such contempt he is discharged from being one of the Capital Burgesses." On 22nd June, 1742, a member was discharged for "not attending and doeing the duty of a capital burgess for many years past." It would seem that verbal notice only was given for the meetings of the Corporation, which might explain absences, for in 1813 it was ordered that notice be given in writing to every member when a Common Hall was required and that the notice must state the object of the meeting.

Probably there are few towns even today where it can be said that members of local authorities do not reveal the decisions made in Committee and the trend of the debate ; in 1716 the matter was dealt with by the following resolution : "Ordered that noe member of this Hall doe discuss any discourse that happens in the Hall about the affairs of the Corporation or any orders that shall be made at any tyme in the Hall to any person or persons upon payne of being censured by the Hall for their betraing the secrets of the Corporation and it is likewise ordered that such person as shall make knowne to the Hall of any member that shall discover the secrets of the Hall shall have for every such discovery five shillings."

Robes were worn by the members ; they were required in 1668 to obtain them by a given date, under penalty of ten shillings, and on 1st August, 1726, an order was made requiring the wearing of robes at every meeting.

On 1st August, 1780, it having been suggested that Innkeepers were excluded from election as a capital burgess by some order made previously at meetings of the Common Hall, it was decided to revoke it.

The Corporation Act of 1661 compelled all Mayors, Aldermen, Bailiffs, Town Clerks and others connected with the government of cities and boroughs to take, in addition to the oaths of Allegiance and Supremacy, an oath declaring it to be unlawful to take arms against the King and denouncing the oath called "The Solemn League and Covenant," and to take the Sacrament of the Lord's Supper according to the rites of the Church of England. The Corporation records contain several certificates testifying that the law had been complied with in this respect, but on 17th April, 1732, a person who had neglected to take the Sacrament in due time and was therefore not qualified to take his seat as a capital burgess was re-elected.

It would be illegal today to pay a pension to members of the Council whose financial circumstances had deteriorated. It appears to have been customary to do so in the seventeenth century, for in 1696 it was decided to grant a pension to a member who had "fallen to decay, it being usual in most Cities and Corporations that where any of the magistrates by reason of age or otherwise it doth soe happen, that they be allowed a pension from the city or towne," so a pension of ten shillings a year for the rest of his natural life was granted, payable in instalments on the usual quarter days. Another pension, twenty shillings per annum payable in quarterly instalments, was granted in 1707 to a former capital burgess ''now being decayed in his estate.''

From the date of Queen Elizabeth's charter until 1835 the capital burgesses were self-elected ; the burgesses had no say in the matter. The Municipal Corporations Act, 1835, established the right of election by the burgesses, but it would seem that the retiring members of the old governing body had some doubt as to the ability of the burgesses to make the best use of the new power given to them, for on 11th December, 1835, prior to the first municipal election under the Act, the Bailiffs were requested to call a public meeting in order to submit to the burgesses a list of persons qualified to be elected councillors, and to recommend to them, if thought advisable, a list of persons for their choice, and to consider the best mode of electing them.

Prior to the incorporation of the Borough, there were four High Bailiffs, two for the Staffordshire part of the town and two for the Warwickshire part. The charter of 1560 authorised the election of two Bailiffs. Their names are recorded with those of the capital burgesses in the minute books, but no indication is given as to who presided at the meetings of the Common Hall. It would seem that one of the Bailiffs represented the Staffordshire side, and the other the Warwickshire side, as a minute of 1779 stated that it was the custom for the Bailiff in the Staffordshire part of Tamworth to pay the expenses of the Easter Court Leet ; no doubt, in any case, there were certain duties required to be performed separately, such as the payment of the fee-farm rent.

The charter required the election of the Bailiffs to take place between 9 a.m. and 12 noon on the first day of August. On 1st August, 1824, ''the Reverend Robert Watkin Lloyd paid the fine of twenty pounds (the maximum penalty payable by any member refusing to accept the office of Bailiff) to be excused from serving the office of Bailiff, to which office he was nominated this day according to the usual Rule of Rotation.'' It might be thought that this reference to rotation implied selection according to length of service, as often happens today, but this was not the case during the first half of the nineteenth century for the minute book reveals that on several occasions the persons elected as Bailiffs had been elected only the same day as Capital Burgesses. It seems strange that a newcomer should be elected to the important office of Bailiff as one would have thought that small though the duties were compared to those of the Mayor today, some experience as a capital burgess would be desirable.

Two chamberlains to take care of the town's finances were appointed by the Court Leet until the borough was incorporated, when they were elected annually with the Bailiffs. In 1689 it was decided to appoint four chamberlains, two from the Capital Burgesses and two from the inhabitants ; this system continued for eighteen years and then the election of two from the inhabitants was discontinued. At a later date a practice of appointing the retiring bailiffs as chamberlains was adopted.

Control of the chamberlains' accounts was probably restricted to production of the account book at meetings of the corporate body, for the minutes occasionally show that the chamberlains handed in their accounts upon expiration of office. The balance in hand must have been produced also, for it was noted on 16th August, 1695, that "the towne box being opened this day there is found in it the sum of £11. 14s. 6d." In November, 1708, "Mr. Homer, the surviving chamberlain, Mr. Knight being dead, gave up his accounts as chamberlain for the year ended 1st August last upon which it appeared that he had received £59. 16s. 3d. and that he had paid £67. 1s. 9d. so that Mr. Bradgate (one of the retiring bailiffs) paid Mr. Homer £7. 5s. 6d. to balance the accounts." This might suggest that Mr. Bradgate was generous enough to provide the money out of his own pocket, but the bailiffs had a source of revenue of their own which did not find its way into the chamberlains' accounts. This was the income from fairs and the market tolls. In 1753 the capital burgesses ordered the chamberlains to pay the fee-farm rent to the Crown out of their box, any usage or custom to the contrary notwithstanding, because the expenses of the bailiffs had increased by reason of the decrease in the tolls and other franchises belonging to them. At a later date some allowance must have been paid to the bailiffs, for in 1817 it was ordered that it should be withdrawn and that instead they were to be reimbursed the sum necessarily expended in the execution of their office.

Another indication of the retention of market tolls by the Bailiffs is given in a minute of 1704, when they provided new stalls at a cost of £10, and it was agreed that the sum should be paid out of the "town box," that each of the two bailiffs should pay ten shillings, and that their successors should pay a similar sum until the original charge plus interest had been repaid, the bailiffs to leave the stalls in good repair at the end of their year of office.

In 1690, ex-bailiff Harding having refused to pay the fee-farm rent while in office, "which may forfeit the liberties and privileges that the inhabitants on the Staffordshire side have by that payment" it was ordered that he be proceeded against by complaint to the Lord Chief Justice. Presumably he paid up, as there is no further entry, but a previous minute suggests that the payment should have been made out of the profits of St. George's Fair.

In 1686, in deciding that the bellman or constable be continued as formerly, it was added that the bailiffs and capital burgesses desired that a contribution should be made through the town for him. Sometimes a direct charge was imposed on some of the inhabitants, as instanced in the repair of pumps and wells which were attended to by well-wardens : in 1696 it was ordered "that the chamberlains do pay to Isaiah Orton the sum of thirty shillings towards the discharge of repairing the pumps at Harding's well, the whole charge being forty shillings, and that the rest be paid by the inhabitants by a levie to be collected within the precincts of the said well." It was also ordered, to put things right for the future, "that the chamberlains do discharge the bills of whatsoever works shall be done under the ground in any of the public pumps within this town and that the well wardens as often as there shall be any occasion for repairs do first make it known to the chamberlains before they set any to work or anything that shall be wanting under ground and that what charge shall happen to be in repairing above ground be at the charge of the inhabitants within the precincts of such pumps."

The income of the Corporation was small, and apart from any special levy, there was no charge by way of a rate. It was not until 1836 that a general power was given to boroughs to levy a "borough rate," and then it was collected by the overseers of the poor as part of the poor rate. The first borough rate was one shilling in the pound.

The bailiffs and the capital burgesses did themselves well on every possible occasion when they could justify a celebration of some national or local event ; every opportunity was taken. For instance, upon the proclamation of King William and Queen Mary in 1689 a stage was erected in the market place, and two hogsheads of ale were put at the disposal of "such gentlemen as the bailiffs might think fit to treat" ; six weeks later, "in order to manifest our great satisfaction and rejoyceing for the happy coronation," six pounds was used out of the "town store." At the proclamation of Queen Anne, five pounds was spent in twelve bottles of claret to drink the Queen's health, and in ale and tobacco. The victory over the French and the Spaniards in 1702 called for half-a-hogshead of the best ale and six shillings worth of cakes. The cost of proclaiming Queen Anne was more than at her coronation, claret being excluded at the latter celebration and fifteen shillings being spent on ale and tobacco. The proclamation of King George in 1714, however, was celebrated like that of Queen Anne, and suggests a standard form of celebration at proclamations. By a minute of 21st January, 1687, it was ordered "that the doe eating be referred to the bailiffs to appoint the place where it shall be eaten by the company (the corporate body), and that the keeper's fee for the doe be paid by the chamberlains," but no indication is given as to what they were celebrating.

The arrangements made for meeting a debt in 1786 are inter-esting. In 1765 the capital burgesses had to mortgage property in Market Street to produce £120 then remaining owing after their persistence in contesting at law the claims of the Repingtons to nominate the Vicars of the parish, referred to in the chapter dealing with the Parish Church. In 1786 it was decided to pay off the mortgage by a unique method which showed that some of the capital burgesses were public-spirited : ten of them advanced the sum of nine pounds each, and six the sum of five pounds each, all without payment of interest, to be repaid by means of a draw to be held annually on the day the bailiffs were to be elected, to such four of the subscribers whose names should be then drawn, those who had advanced more than one share of five pounds to be "entitled to be paid what he or they lend above one share before he or they who lend one share only, or in case any of the subscribers should depart this life before he or they are repaid what he or they have advanced and lent, his or their heirs executors or administrators shall be entitled to the sum advanced and unpaid at the next Lammas Day after such decease, as not more than £20 shall be paid in any one year without the consent of the Chamberlains and the major part of the then unpaid subscribers.'' A further interesting point about this arrangement is that the Reverend Simon Collins, who was the party affected by the dispute with the Repingtons, was one of the subscribers, and was therefore lending a sum towards the deficiency which had arisen through his own persistence in the matter, twenty-five years after his claim had been dismissed. He was a capital burgess at the time of the dispute, in fact from 1755 until his death in 1793, and was elected as one of the Bailiffs on four separate occasions.

The amount of business transacted by the old corporate body was very small. Indeed, apart from the annual meeting on the first day of August for the election of the bailiffs only two or three meetings were held in the course of the year. Business was confined to the election of officers, the care of corporate property, the control of the Saturday market and the town's watchmen, encroachments on highways and the making of an occasional byelaw or regulation. The committee system was not commenced until 1837 (probably then because the Act of 1835 authorised the appointment of committees) when it was decided to appoint a Watch Committee and an Estate Committee for the superintendence and management of the rights and property of the Corporation, including the cleansing of the streets, roads and bridges, with full power for any three of them to act.

On 1st February, 1865, a deputation from a public meeting of ratepayers attended the Council meeting and presented a resolution which they had passed, ''That the meetings of the Town Council in future be open to the public.'' The Council promised that the subject should be considered, and on the 3rd of May following they granted the request. This publicity, long before the time (1908) when the press was admitted by law to Council meetings, enabled the *Tamworth Herald* in 1870 to give the following impression : ''The reports of the Town Council meetings are more like reports of convocations held in Billingsgate, than the utterances of a number of sane men, and I suppose every member of the Council prides himself on being perfectly conscious. Yet what undignified exhibitions they make of themselves ! How unparliamentary their observations are to one another ! Happy are those who are out of the Borough of Tamworth. The manner in which the Council meetings are conducted is a disgrace to civilisation.''

It is an indication of the extent to which local government has developed during the past century, or since 1835 if that year of municipal reform is taken as a landmark, to record that the powers and duties of the Council of the Borough now include the following : the control of the Market, the Public Library, the Cemetery, the Public Baths, Allotments, Hackney Carriages, the Civic Restaurant, the Castle and the Pleasure Grounds, and the large corporate estate including the various housing estates ; the repair, improvement and cleansing of highways, the making-up and adoption of private streets, sewerage and drainage, the removal of house refuse, public health nuisances, the inspection of meat and slaughterhouses, the provision of parking places, the making and operation of many byelaws, including those relating to good rule and government of the town and the construction of new buildings, and, under delegation of powers from the County Council, town planning and civil defence. The list is a brief one, for it would require a long and detailed catalogue to show the wide variety of matters administered by the local governing body today.

CHAPTER XI

LOCAL GOVERNMENT DURING THE WAR

A MUNICIPAL HISTORY OF TAMWORTH would be incomplete if it did not refer to the part which local government played in the second World War. During the war of 1914-18 local authorities were not called upon by the central government to undertake any major special functions. Such war-time duties as were then carried out, were very insignificant compared with those in the last war, when the responsibilities of local councils entered an entirely new sphere. For the first time in history they were called upon to play a prominent part in Home Defence. They responded to the call in a magnificent way, performing tasks of which they had had no previous experience, and making a material contribution to the national effort of bringing the war to a successful conclusion by being ready to preserve the lives and homes of the civilian population as much as possible, thus maintaining the public morale.

It was in 1935 that the Government, owing to the international situation, called the attention of local authorities to the need for taking precautionary measures to safeguard the civil population against attack by enemy aircraft in time of war. The major responsibility for preparing such plans was placed on County Councils and County Boroughs, but all county district councils were required by law to assist and to carry out such duties as might be delegated to them by the county council. The Tamworth Borough Council, in its responsibility to the Staffordshire County Council, prepared a scheme ; not an easy task, as no one had any experience of the effects of air attacks, or as to the measures which could be of any value to assist the public in what promised to be a new stage in modern warfare.

Gradually a scheme emerged, but recruitment of the personnel necessary to operate the services proposed to be established was very slow, as was the case throughout the country, owing to the views of many people that war was not likely to happen, that if it did come it would be soon enough to volunteer at the last moment, or that in any case nothing much could be done about it as no really effective measures could be taken against air attack. Fortunately, there were those who did come forward as volunteers and so helped to lay the foundations of the Civil Defence Service which operated in the town when war eventually came in 1939.

It had been anticipated that air attack might mean the dropping of gas bombs as well as high explosive and incendiaries. Consequently before the war there was a feverish assembly, in a local factory, of the component parts of gas masks or respirators, and these were distributed by the newly-formed Warden Service to all the inhabitants of the town, necessitating visits to all households to fit and deliver the right size.

Local plans were similar to those in other towns, but should be placed on record. The town was divided into sectors, served by "wardens' posts" at which the wardens carried out their duties when not on patrol, and to which they were required to report any incidents. Their training and duties included the reporting of air raid damage, keeping in touch with the people in their sectors, advising the public in the care and use of gas respirators and the kinds and effects of war gases, the extinguishing of incendiary bombs and the evacuation of the public from their homes in the event of damage or the fall of unexploded bombs.

First aid parties were formed and thoroughly trained in first aid so that they could treat injuries received from incendiary, high explosive and gas bombs. A Rescue Service was trained so as to be able to rescue persons trapped in damaged buildings, and to make safe any dangerous buildings. Eventually these two services were combined, and, at a later stage in the war, gave valuable service in transporting wounded soldiers from special trains to emergency hospitals. A First Aid Depot for these parties was established at the Baths in the Castle Pleasure Grounds. A First Aid Post, ready to deal with such cases of injury as need not be sent to a hospital, was set up at the School of Industry in Marmion Street. Services were also arranged to "decontaminate" roads and buildings in the event of gas being used, to clear roads of debris, and to carry out speedily any repair necessary to maintain traffic routes.

A Report and Control Centre was created at the Assembly Rooms to receive air raid warnings and to control the various services, and a messenger service, which included long-distance motor-cycle despatch riders, was attached to the centre. Provision was also made for assistance to be received from, or given to, other towns in the event of air attacks taking place on a large scale.

All these services were manned more or less continuously, being strengthened by members who reported for duty immediately upon the receipt of an air raid warning. The Control Centre, however, was in operation night and day from the beginning until the end of the war.

It was expected that the proximity of Tamworth to Birmingham might result in many air raids, and plans had to be prepared upon this basis. Although the town had many warnings, it was spared the fate which befell so many. Tamworth was indeed fortunate, for notwithstanding the raids suffered elsewhere in the Midlands and the passage of enemy aircraft over the town so frequently, bombs fell within the Borough on only four occasions. Six high explosive bombs were dropped in the Fazeley Road area on the night of 16th September, 1940, causing window damage only ; twenty-five incendiary bombs fell near the Railway Station later the same night, and fifty in the vicinity of Alders Mills on 21st October, 1940. The Corporation housing estate at Manor Road, Bolehall, had a narrow escape on the night of 16th and 17th May, 1941, when three high explosive bombs fell. It was remarkable that no lives were lost in that raid, nor were any persons injured or houses destroyed, although 98 houses were slightly damaged.

The sirens sounded the air raid warning in the town on 138 occasions, but in addition 658 preliminary warnings not followed by the sounding of the siren were received. The longest period of warning lasted twelve hours and three minutes, from 6.23 p.m. to 6.26 a.m., and the shortest lasted two minutes. The longest period during which warnings were received on consecutive nights was at the end of August, 1940, when the sirens sounded on eight nights.

Altogether 985 persons, including 269 women, entered the Civil

Defence Services of the town during the war. The highest number in the Services at any one time was 426, including 56 women. These figures do not include those enrolled in the Fire Brigade Auxiliary Service, which was administered as a national service, nor do they include the large number recruited for fire prevention duties for service under the local authority.

In connection with fire prevention, a new duty was imposed upon the Borough Council, that of registering local inhabitants for compulsory duties. The local Fire Brigade had been taken over by the Government in the early stages of the war as part of a National Fire Service. In December, 1940, owing to the policy of the enemy in using the incendiary bomb form of attack, "Supplementary Fire Parties" were formed to serve under the direction of the local authority. Nearly a thousand volunteers enrolled and were allocated to areas in the town in which they were called upon to assist in the event of incendiary bomb attack. On 3rd February, 1941, Tamworth, by reason of its situation, was selected as an area in which all business premises were to be safeguarded from such form of attack, and the Regional Commissioner appointed by the Government issued an Order requiring every occupier of such property to make arrangements, whether by himself or by a joint scheme with his neighbours, for the purpose of securing that fires occurring at the premises as a result of hostile attack would be immediately detected and combated, and making it obligatory for all male persons between the ages of 18 and 60 working at such premises to undertake fire prevention duties there, unless legally exempted. Each factory or group of business premises had its centre where the employees were required to perform fire-guard duties during the night. Six months later further Orders were issued by the Regional Commissioner requiring all males between those ages to be registered by the Borough Council for compulsory fire prevention duties. It became the duty of the Council to train these persons and to allocate them to fire guard parties in the various streets in the Borough to supplement those who had volunteered for such duties. This was a most unpleasant task, and the Council endeavoured to get the Orders revoked, but without success. Later, the age limit for males was extended to 63, and women between the ages of 20 and 40 also became liable for duty. Although 5,090 persons were registered, the majority were able to claim exemption from street fire-guard duties on the ground that they were already performing such duties at their place of work, or on the ground of ill-health, leaving only 1,543 persons for allocation to duties. Night duty had to be performed on a rota basis at a fixed centre, supplemented by the general body of volunteer fire-guards upon the sounding of the siren. This compulsory standing-by on night duty, both at the business premises and at the local authority's fire guard centre, was regarded by all concerned as a waste of time, and certainly it would have been a much better arrangement for fire-guards to have done their duty under the direction of the Fire Brigade Service at fewer and selected premises, than under the time-wasting and inadequate arrangements which the Council were compelled by law to administer.

Another duty of the Borough Council during the war was the billeting of women and children who came to Tamworth for safety from air raids. An "Evacuation Scheme" had been prepared by the Government for the dispersal, in the event of war, of women and children from densely populated areas and coastal towns to such inland areas and towns on the west coast as were considered to be less vulnerable to air attack. Tamworth was scheduled as a reception area. A protest by the Council on the ground that the town was near to Birmingham and likely to be involved in air raids met with no success ; they were told that the vulnerability of coastal towns made it necessary to use areas in the country and that these were limited because of the necessity to consider the suitability of local authority services for receiving additional population. So, before the war began, a survey of all houses in the town had to be made to ascertain which homes could receive evacuees either voluntarily or compulsorily, and billeting officers recruited from the Women's Voluntary Services were appointed in readiness. The persons included in parties from the "evacuation areas" were children sent as a complete school unit with their teachers, children under school age accompanied by their mothers, expectant mothers, the aged and the infirm.

Notwithstanding the survey carried out, it was anticipated that if and when billeting had to take place, the circumstances in many cases would have altered, and that it would also depend on how the parties were constituted, as to age and sex, if the billeting arrangements were to be carried out smoothly. The billeting organisation was destined to be tested almost immediately upon the outbreak of war, for on 6th September, 1939, three days after the war commenced, a contingent of 557 children arrived from West Bromwich; nevertheless all were billeted, without recourse to compulsion, in about two hours. Within a month, however, one-third of this number had returned home, and by Christmas of that year nearly all the children had gone back. This was due to the "phoney" stage of the war, there being as yet no air attacks, and particularly to the proximity of the evacuation area to the reception area, as many of the children went home at week-ends, thus defeating the purpose of the scheme, on the curious assumption that it was safe to be at home from Friday to Monday but not so during the rest of the week. The children therefore became discontented, and gradually drifted home for good.

A special train arrived on Sunday afternoon, 2nd June, 1940, bringing a party of 518 women and children, evacuees from Broadstairs on the south-east coast. Again billeting was successfully carried out in about two hours. Most of the members of this party remained in Tamworth until the end of the war.

On 26th October, 1940, a party of 294 mothers and children arrived from London. This party included persons of many nationalities who had been living in London : French, Belgians, Italians and Austrians. Unlike the other parties, it included many large families, with the result that billeting was not easy. Several of the families had to be accommodated for a week or two in the Congregational Schoolroom in Aldergate while a few vacant houses, which had been closed just before the war, were requisitioned by the Council, re-opened and repaired sufficiently to make them habitable. The Londoners did not settle down well. No doubt Tamworth was too quiet for them after being used to city life.

A fourth party of evacuees, 81 children, arrived from Liverpool on 16th May, 1941. In addition to these parties which were officially planned by the Government, other arrangements were made for the reception of individual children from various parts of the country. In all, 2,581 women and children were billeted in 1,200 homes in the Borough during the war, the highest number remaining in the town at any one time being 952.

The evacuation scheme brought many problems, as it was bound to do. Some of the parties were made up entirely of children from the same schools, but many missed their parents even though they had their own school friends. It required considerable patience upon the part of their temporary foster-mothers to cope with sick and difficult children, and it was to the credit of the families who received these war-time guests into their homes that billeting proceeded so smoothly as it did. There were, of course, householders who complained that the evacuees were "difficult," there were evacuees who complained that householders were equally difficult, exchanges of billets had to be made when complaints arose, children sometimes ran away or caused trouble, relatives of children had to be traced, letters from anxious parents of the unaccompanied children had to be answered by the householders or by the welfare officers, clothing had often to be supplied to supplement that possessed by the children, additional bedding had to be distributed, gifts of furniture had to be obtained to furnish the empty requisitioned houses : these are only a few of the problems which had to be faced. The Government allowances paid to the householders could not adequately recompense the hosts who, in the generosity of their natures, treated their guests as members of their own families. Although the local authority had power by law to resort to compulsory billeting, it was unnecessary to use it ; a Billeting Appeals Tribunal was set up to hear appeals by householders or evacuees, but in spite of the many problems only two appeals were made, one by a householder and the other by an evacuee.

Many a child may have owed its life to being away from its native town when bombs fell ; the householders of Tamworth played their part in the national war-time effort by giving shelter and food to those who came here for safety.

During the war, local authorities had the power to establish "British Restaurants" to provide meals, primarily for war workers. Such a restaurant was set up by the Borough Council in a building in Lichfield Street which, a century earlier, had been used by Sir Robert Peel as a school. After the war, when local authorities were given power to continue such restaurants as "Civic Restaurants," this restaurant was moved to the Assembly Rooms, where a room was adapted for the purpose.

One good feature of the war-time arrangements was the establishment of the organisation known as the Women's Voluntary Services (the "W.V.S.") which rendered valuable assistance in connection with billeting and rest centres. In fact, it proved to be so useful that it has continued ever since as a peace-time body, and is still giving generous help in all kinds of voluntary work in the town.

Chapter XII

THE FUTURE DEVELOPMENT OF TAMWORTH

THE DEVELOPMENT OF LOCAL GOVERNMENT ADMINISTRATION to the form in which we see it today has taken place, not only in Tamworth but elsewhere, within the last century and a half. The industrial revolution had its effect upon the social conditions of the country, and the rapidly changing circumstances demanded the provision of new public services as well as the creation of democratic, in place of self-elected, local bodies. Up to the middle of the nineteenth century the powers and duties of local authorities were very few. It is not surprising that the absence of legislation to control the actions of individuals resulted in the development of towns in a form which affected health and public amenities for generations. In former days, as now, a burgess might be prevented from encroaching with his private property on the public highway, but otherwise he could erect buildings as he chose without regard to the health or convenience of anyone else. It was not until the second half of the nineteenth century that local authorities had the power to make byelaws for the purpose of ensuring that new dwellinghouses and other buildings conformed to certain standards in the interests of those who were to live or work in them, and to ensure that they were constructed of such materials and in such a manner as would give safety. Even then it was not possible, provided that the building complied with the byelaws in respect of such matters as materials and construction, to prevent the erection of premises which might become an obstruction or interfere with public amenities ; factories could be erected immediately adjacent to dwellinghouses, and houses could be built in a position which would obviously and seriously prevent future development.

It is well for us to remember, therefore, when we are tempted to criticise the way in which a locality may have developed, that the powers of a local authority in those days were extremely limited, and that it was not until town planning was introduced that conditions began to improve. Even then the new powers were adoptive and not compulsory, and Tamworth did not adopt planning control until 1935.

Until comparatively recent times, the development of Tamworth has been slow. For centuries the boundaries of the Borough remained unaltered and even when rates were eventually levied, the income therefrom was low, as the town had insufficient rateable value to develop public services to the extent which it otherwise could have done. When Sir Robert Peel cut the first turf on the Staffordshire Moor to herald the introduction of the railway, he spoke of the great developments which it would bring to the town, but it cannot be said that this really came true, although the town has progressed in a quiet manner, and, within the last thirty years, far more rapidly than before.

Apart from the private development in the Leys (which is an illustration of the lack of planning control in earlier days), the various Corporation housing estates made a large contribution to the expansion of the town. From 1929 until the outbreak of war, a real step forward was made in civic development. The enlargement and transformation of the Castle Pleasure Grounds, the provision of an open-air swimming pool and other amenities in the grounds, the extension of boundaries with consequent expansion in the added areas, and a continuous programme for the removal of insanitary houses, all played their part in making visible alterations and improvements in the Borough.

Town planning was first brought into the legislation of this country by the passing of a Housing and Town Planning Act in 1909. Although this was amended by further Acts, little progress was made generally throughout the country until 1932, when planning powers were extended. This Act, however, was adoptive like its predecessors, but the Borough Council decided to operate it.

As a result of this step they were able to control future development within certain limits, pending the preparation of a town planning scheme. The second World War made it difficult to proceed with a scheme, although "interim development" could continue to be controlled. After the war a new Act was passed, whereby town planning became compulsory instead of adoptive, but it made County Councils and County Boroughs the planning authorities. In consequence, Tamworth Borough Council ceased to be a planning authority, and the Staffordshire County Council took over the responsibility of preparing a planning scheme for the Borough, although they delegated limited powers in respect of interim development to the Borough Council.

A planning scheme has now been prepared, and this will guide and control the future development of the Borough. In common with such schemes elsewhere it will, among other things, establish zones for residential, industrial and agricultural uses, designate new and improved highways, and preserve open spaces. One of the matters provided for in the scheme is the construction of a new by-pass road which will run from Fazeley Road to Bonehill Road, across the River Tame in Lichfield Road, then over the Staffordshire Moor and the railway, skirting the Girls' High School and emerging at the junction of Comberford, Wigginton and Ashby Roads, for the purpose of relieving Upper Gungate, Aldergate, Silver Street and Lady Bridge from the increasing traffic passing through the Borough from Ashby and Nottingham to Birmingham. A new road will also link Fazeley Road with Bolehall and Kettlebrook across the Castle Pleasure Grounds.

The town has received much benefit in recent years from works carried out by the Trent River Board. The construction of a channel west of Lady Bridge and the removal of obstructions from the river have reduced the risk of danger from floods, which in former times caused much damage in the town.

Before the second World War the Council adopted the policy of purchasing properties surrounding Middle Entry, with the object of providing better communication between Market Street and George Street. In 1805 the Council had been successful in obtaining the co-operation of Lord Townshend, to whom the property then belonged, in creating a public passageway. Unfortunately the outbreak of war caused the scheme of development to be post-poned. After the war, however, further properties were purchased in readiness for the development of this area. Some of the build-ings having been demolished, the Saturday street market, which for centuries has occupied the Market Place near the Town Hall, was transferred on 3rd May, 1958, to this area, which will thus become the new Market Place, and in course of time other premises will be taken down and a new shopping centre will be made. The develop-ment already carried out has enabled the beautiful Parish Church to be viewed with advantage from new angles, and the setting of the Church has been much improved by the recent demolition of Old School Yard on the west, giving a new and spacious vehicular entrance, known as St. Editha's Close, which also affords a better view of the west entrance and the tower. It is also intended to widen Church Street in front of the Church by the removal of part of the churchyard, and a proposal of the Corporation to transform the remainder of the churchyard into a Garden of Rest similar to Aldergate Cemetery will make a considerable improvement, and be of much benefit to the public.

Another scheme of development which will create a new feature will be the erection of flats at the lower end of Bolebridge Street, overlooking the River Anker and the Castle Pleasure Grounds. It is proposed to construct a riverside walk which will be extended eventually from Bolebridge to Common Lane.

A programme of slum clearance, to cover a period of nine years and involving the demolition of about 500 houses, will add to the transformation which has been proceeding during the past thirty years.

What will have the biggest influence in the development of the town is a decision which has been made by the Council to increase the population of the Borough from 13,000 to 20,000 by housing people from Birmingham. In view of its importance in the future history of Tamworth, it is desirable to place on record how this plan has evolved.

About twenty years ago, consideration was given by a Royal Commission to the problem of the ever-increasing industries and populations of the large cities, and upon the publication of the Commission's report in 1940 the Government made arrangements for the preparation of reports on what were called, to use an ugly description, "conurbations" : these included the West Midlands. A report was issued in 1947 recommending, firstly, the fixing of a "green belt," in which development would be severely restricted in order to prevent the further encroachment of Birmingham and other large towns in the West Midlands upon the surrounding countryside, and, secondly, the distribution of excess population and industry to small towns, the proposal having the double intention of relieving congestion in the one case and of creating desirable expansion in the other.

In the report it was recommended that the Borough of Tamworth should receive "overspill" population from Birmingham to the extent of bringing the population of the town up to 20,000.

The policy of restricting the growth of the large towns was accepted by the Government, and the report on the West Midlands was recommended by it to the Planning Authorities in connection with the Development Plans which they were required to prepare under the Town and Country Planning Act, 1947. The Staffordshire County Council, being the planning authority for Tamworth, agreed with the Borough Council that the proposal to transfer population and industry from Birmingham to Tamworth should be accepted. The Tamworth Borough Council, in pursuance of this decision, have entered into an agreement with the Birmingham City Council and the Staffordshire County Council whereby they have undertaken to erect 1,700 houses during a period of ten years. The major part of this development will take place in the area to the west of Comberford Road.

As it is undesirable that population should be removed from Birmingham to live in Tamworth only to return to the city daily for their work, arrangements are being made for new industries to be accommodated on land in Lichfield Road ; a site has been acquired by the Corporation for this purpose, and it is likely that it will be extended when circumstances demand it.

The acceptance of overspill population from Birmingham will be the most important development which has ever taken place in the history of Tamworth. It will be the largest increase the town has ever known, for the population has not varied much during the greater part of a century, except by the extension of boundaries. It will bring a new era of development in building, industry and commercial enterprise, and will also give greater opportunity for the provision of civic and other amenities.

The Borough is also likely to be affected in the next few years by a further extension of boundaries. There is every prospect that the urban parishes surrounding the town will be brought within the Borough. Like many other small towns, Tamworth has suffered during the past century because its rateable value has been insufficient to expand the public services and to provide new amenities, and it should benefit by the modern view that the areas administered by local authorities should be large enough to make them economic units. Tamworth is now in the process of transformation to an extent which has never happened before in its long history ; it is not living in its past, important though that may be. The town and the surrounding district have everything to gain, and nothing to lose, by the creation of a local government unit for the whole area capable of having resources sufficient to provide new or improved services and additional amenities which would benefit the whole of the local community.

Tamworth can look forward with confidence to the future, even though it cannot regain the importance it acquired when it was the capital of Mercia twelve hundred years ago. Opportunities are now arising which can, given boldness and courage, lead to an era of prosperous development, whilst preserving such of the characteristics of the town as link it with an historic past.

LOCAL TOPOGRAPHY

as revealed by translations of the
Court Leet Rolls and other documents
in the possession of the Corporation.

Aldergate :   Elregate, 1294 ; Ellergate, 1347 ; Eldergate, 1422.

Anker :   Oncur, 1294.

Bitterscote :   Bytterescote, 1358 ; Byteruscote, 1363.

Bolebridge :   Bollebrugge, 1316.

Bolebridge Street :   Bollebruggestrete, 1316.

Bonehill :   Bollenhull, 1290.

Bradfords :   Bradeford, 1290 ; Bradefordstrete, 1318.

Brewery Lane :   Wyburne lane, 1318.

Church Lane :   Schoolmaster's lane, 1384.

Church Street :   (west) High Street, 1295, 1389, 1439.
Chirchestrete, 1391 ; le Cherchestrete,
1407 ; Chyrchestrete, 1418.

Colehill :   Crossestrete, 1381.

College Lane :   Cocket's lane, 1314.

Common Lane :   Agatewater leader, 1297 ; Egate, 1316.

Fazeley :   Faresley, 1358 ; Faseley, 1700.

George Street :   Bulstake strete, 1424.

Hopwas :   Hopewas, 1319.

Kettlebrook :   Ketulbroke, 1440.

Lady Bridge :   Bridge of Our Lady, 1294 ; Ladybrugge,
1355 ; St. Mary's Bridge, 1470.

Lichfield Street :	(east) Lichefeldestrete, 1369 ; Lychefeld-strete, 1384.
	(west) Otewellestrete, 1290 ; Otewalle-strete, 1314.
Little Church Lane :	Chirchelone, 1337.
Lower Gungate :	Gumpiyat, 1289 ; Gumpigate, 1290.
Mill Lane :	Dead lane, 1697.
Moor Street :	Moor lane, 1470.
Perrycrofts :	Pericroft, 1290.
St. John Street :	Castle lane, 1457.
Salters Lane :	Salterslone, 1294.
Silver Street :	Ladybruggestrete, 1354.
Spinning School Lane :	Schoolhouse lane, 1697.
Upper Gungate :	Stony lane, 1697.

STREETS, PLACES AND DESCRIPTIONS NO LONGER IN EXISTENCE

Bulstake, 1314 ; Bolestake, 1363 ; Bulstakewell, 1508. (George Street cross-roads.)

Butchery, 1442.

Carrefour, 1314 ; Carfax, 1347 ; Quarfoukes, 1295. (Silver Street cross-roads.)

Catteslone (Cat Lane), 1319 ; Priestlone, 1460 ; Catt Lane, 1684.

Castel orchard, 1390.

Cross, 1363 ; Stonecross, 1293, 1516 ; le stonen cros, 1365.

Cuckingstool, 1563.

Deyne (Dean) Pool, 1510.

Kyngesdych, 1378.

Pillory, 1294, 1563.

Spyttulfyld, 1431.

Swynemarket, 1388.

Walfurlong, 1295.

TABLE

showing the population and number of houses since the first Census.

	Population			No. of Houses		
	Staffs.	*Warwick*	*Total*	*Staffs.*	*Warwick.*	*Total*
1801	1,154	1,632	2,786	228	317	545
1811	1,327	1,664	2,991	263	318	581
1821	1,636	1,938	3,574	324	393	717
1831	1,711	1,826	3,537	338	391	729
1841	1,797	1,992	3,789	362	419	781
1851	1,915	2,144	4,059	375	461	836
1861	1,989	2,337	4,326	449	497	946
1871	2,351	2,238	4,589	512	505	1,017
1881	2,589	2,302	4,891	560	510	1,070
1891	6,614	—	6,614	1,344	—	1,344
1901	7,271	—	7,271	1,526	—	1,526
1911	7,378	—	7,378	1,694	—	1,694
1921	8,032	—	8,032	1,694	—	1,694
1931	7,510	—	7,510	1,884	—	1,884
1932	11,711	—	11,711	2,725	—	2,725
1951	12,889	—	12,889	3,688	—	3,688

Note : The Borough was extended in 1890 and 1932.
The figures for 1932 are taken from the 1931 census.

Area (acres)

			Staffs.	*Warwick.*	*Total*
31st March, 1889	...	...	150	50	200
1st April, 1889 ...	...	...	200	—	200
1st November, 1890	...	...	285	—	285
1st April, 1932 ...	...	...	2,678	—	2,678

BIBLIOGRAPHY

GENERAL WORKS

Anglo-Saxon Chronicle ; trans., with an introduction by G. H. Garmonsway, Dent, 1953. (Everyman edition.)

Green, J. R.   "A Short History of the English People," J. M. Dent & Sons Ltd., 1874.

Smellie, K. B.   "A History of Local Government," George Allen and Unwin Ltd., 1946.

Stenton, D. M.   "English Society in the early Middle Ages," Penguin Books Ltd., 1951.

Stenton, F. M.   "Anglo-Saxon England," Oxford University Press, second ed., 1947, R.P. 1950.

Vine, J. R. S.   "The English Municipalities, their growth and development," Waterlow & Sons Ltd., 1879.

Whitelock, D.   "The Beginnings of English Society," Penguin Books Ltd.

LOCAL WORKS

Dugdale, W.   "The Antiquities of Warwickshire," Coventry, 1765.

Mitchell, H. C.   "Tamworth Parish Church," Welwyn, Alcuin Pr., 1935.

Mitchell, H. C.   "Tamworth Tower and Town," Tamworth, Woodcock, 1936.

Norris, Rev. H.   "Tamworth Castle," Tamworth, Smith, 1899.

Palmer, C. F. R. "History of the Town and Castle of Tamworth," Tamworth, Thompson, 1875.

Palmer, C. F. R. "History of the Baronial Family of Marmion," Tamworth, Thompson, 1875.

Palmer, C. F. R. "The History and Antiquities of the Collegiate Church of Tamworth, in the County of Stafford," Tamworth, Thompson, 1871.

Roby, J. and H. W. "The History of the Borough and Parish of Tamworth in the Counties of Warwick and Stafford," J. Nichols & Son, 1826.

Shaw, S. "The History and Antiquities of Staffordshire," 1798.

Willington, J. R. "Notes on the Guild of St. George at Tamworth and guild life in England during the Middle Ages," Tamworth, The Herald Co., 1900.

Willington, J. R. "Saint Editha and Tamworth Church," Tamworth, D. Smith, 1896.

INDEX